A New Academic Marketplace

Recent Titles in
Contributions to the Study of Education

Growth of an American Invention: A Documentary History of the Junior and Community College Movement
Thomas Diener

Learning Disability: Social Class and the Construction of Inequality in American Education
James G. Carrier

Policy Controversies in Higher Education
Samuel K. Gove and Thomas M. Stauffer, editors

Effective Education: A Minority Policy Perspective
Charles Vert Willie

Academic Freedom and Catholic Higher Education
James John Annarelli

The University of the Future: The Yugoslav Experience
Miroslav Pečujlić; Tanja Lorković, translator and editor

The Legal Structure of Collective Bargaining in Education
Kenneth H. Ostrander

Partnerships for Improving Schools
Byrd L. Jones and Robert W. Maloy

Teacher Politics: The Influence of Unions
Maurice R. Berube

Toward Black Undergraduate Student Equality in American Higher Education
Michael T. Nettles, editor

The New Servants of Power: A Critique of the 1980s School Reform Movement
Christine M. Shea, Peter Sola, and Ernest Kahane

Social Goals and Educational Reform: American Schools in the Twentieth Century
Charles V. Willie and Inabeth Miller, editors

A New Academic Marketplace

Dolores L. Burke

Foreword by Theodore Caplow

Contributions to the Study of Education
Number 30

Greenwood Press
New York • Westport, Connecticut • London

Library of Congress Cataloging-in-Publication Data

Burke, Dolores L.
   A new academic marketplace / Dolores L. Burke ; foreword by
Theodore Caplow.
      p. cm.—(Contributions to the study of education, ISSN
0196–707X ; no. 30)
   Bibliography: p.
   Includes index.
   ISBN 0–313–26383–3 (lib. bdg. : alk. paper)
      1. College teaching—United States—Case studies. 2. Universities
and colleges—United States—Administration—Case studies.
3. College teachers—United States—Selection and appointment—Case
studies. I. Title. II. Series.
LB2331.B845   1988
378'.125'0973—dc19   88–15445

British Library Cataloguing in Publication Data is available.

Library of Congress Catalog Card Number: 88–15445
ISBN: 0–313–26383–3
ISSN: 0196–707X

First published in 1988

Greenwood Press, Inc.
88 Post Road West, Westport, Connecticut 06881

Printed in the United States of America

(∞)

The paper used in this book complies with the
Permanent Paper Standard issued by the National
Information Standards Organization (Z39.48–1984).

10 9 8 7 6 5 4 3 2 1

Copyright Acknowledgments

Extracts from Dolores L. Burke, "The Academic Marketplace in the 1980s: Appointment
and Termination of Assistant Professors," *The Review of Higher Education* 10:3 (Spring
1987) are used with permission of the publisher.

Extracts from Luther B. Otto and others, *Career Line Prototypes*. Copyright © 1980 by the
Center for the Study of Youth Development. Used with permission.

Contents

Illustrations

Tables

Figures

Foreword

This elegant and instructive book replicates a study on the same topic that was published in 1958 under the title of *The Academic Marketplace*. Reece McGee and I were fortunate as the authors—we enjoyed the writing, the reviews were mostly favorable, and the volume stayed in print for many years. We must again count ourselves as fortunate in having our study so beautifully replicated.

The replication of previous research is the central procedure of empirical science, which relies upon the repetition of experiments and observations to confirm, reject, or modify findings. Replication is more difficult in the social sciences than in the physical sciences because social systems are less easily detached from their historical contexts.

A good sociological replication must copy the base study closely, in order to achieve comparability, while noting at every step how the system under study has been transformed by the passage of time. Dr. Burke performs this balancing feat with brilliant ease, so that it is remarkably easy for her readers to separate the changing from the constant aspects of the academic marketplace in which research universities recruit their faculties.

As the country's major universities became larger, richer, and more bureaucratized over the past three decades, they corrected many of the procedural defects noted in our earlier study. Of the several recommendations we made in 1958, those concerning the equitable treatment of individuals have been largely implemented. There is much less caprice and injustice in the halls of academe than there used to be, and that is reason for rejoicing. Teaching loads and salaries are determined by rule, fringe benefits have been expanded and improved, vacant positions are widely advertised, women and minority candidates are actively sought. The review of candidates' credentials is much more careful, and vacancies are filled in a more orderly and democratic fashion than formerly. Probationary appointments are of adequate length, the criteria for promotion to tenure are explicit, and promotion decisions are hedged with safeguards. Unfair practices that were formerly commonplace, like freezing the salary of a tenured professor, are now rare and actionable.

The continuities are at least as impressive as the changes. A decentralized social system, like American higher education, has enormous inertia with respect to fundamental values and directions. The conflict between the demands of teaching and of research seems as

sharp as ever. The prestige hierarchy of universities and departments—now quantified and quasi-official—still determines which scholarly achievements will be recognized and which will be ignored. The relationship between central administrations and academic departments is still marred by mutual distrust. The management of universities is more orderly than it used to be but not notably more effective.

Like the American manufacturing company that it resembles in some respects, the American university has lost a good deal of its competitive edge vis-à-vis the comparable institutions of other advanced societies. Rigid procedures limit its productivity and its internal constituencies are quick to oppose reform.

Meanwhile, the institution continues to evolve, and will continue to display both continuity and change. The sociologist who undertakes to trace its development twenty or thirty years from now will find that Dr. Burke has built a strong platform from which to climb.

THEODORE CAPLOW

Acknowledgments

This research would not have been possible without the assistance of many people. Chief among them are the respondents themselves—306 faculty members at six major research universities who were willing to share with me their experiences and observations on faculty mobility. The courtesy and cooperation given by these busy professionals provided constant encouragement throughout the project. Gratitude is due, also, to the administrators on each of the six campuses who gave the initial permission for my visits and assisted with the arrangements. The participants remain unnamed to comply with the confidentiality of the original study, conducted in 1958, of which this is a replication.

I am especially grateful to Theodore Caplow, Commonwealth Professor of Sociology at the University of Virginia, and to Reece McGee, Master Teacher and Professor of Sociology at Purdue University, who gave me full access to their original research data and without whose cooperation and encouragement the study would have been impossible to complete in its present form. I owe special thanks to Professor McGee, who shipped the original interviews to me and who responded quickly and helpfully to every question I asked; he also provided specific assistance in modifying the interview guide and advising on interview technique.

I thank Burton R. Clark for generously sending me a typescript draft of his book, *The Academic Life: Small Worlds, Different Worlds* (1987), which corroborated a good deal of my interview data. Thanks also to Robert T. Blackburn, David D. Dill, Duncan MacRae, Jr., Kenneth I. Spenner, William Toombs, and John M. Vernon for their useful comments and encouragement during manuscript preparation.

I am particularly indebted to Terry Sanford, President Emeritus, and H. Keith H. Brodie, M.D., President, of Duke University, who furnished moral and financial support while I was a staff member of the University during the period when this study was in preparation; and to my staff assistant at Duke, Joan Shipman, who did a superb job of transcribing tapes onto disk throughout the spring of 1986, and who worked and worried with me through various stages of preparation.

Finally, my thanks to my family, who chauffered me to and from airports, handled household emergencies during my absences, and generally tolerated the writer at work.

A New Academic Marketplace

1

Background of the Study

> It is characteristic of higher education systems that they are
> strongly influenced by tradition. They display what a biolo-
> gist calls phylogenetic inertia. This is not surprising, for one
> of their functions is to conserve and transmit the cultural
> inheritance. It is characteristic of them, too, that from time to
> time they adjust themselves—sometimes painfully—to the
> social environment which surrounds them.
>
> ERIC LORD ASHBY

This book is about change—or absence of change. Specifically, it is
about change in the academic marketplace—the internal and external
environment of the university that defines the academic labor market.
The book grew out of a study that developed from an interest in Theodore Caplow and Reece McGee's classic chronicling of the academic
personnel process in *The Academic Marketplace*, published in 1958, and a
curiosity as to whether the conditions they observed then would hold
now.

Marketplace had an immediate and strong impact in higher education
circles. Early reviewers regarded the book as "devastating," "disillusion-
ing," a "straightforward and hard-hitting exposé." A later, more thought-
ful review referred to the study as a "significant contribution to the
sociology of complex organization" (Mack 1959). It is the latter context in
which Caplow and McGee's work is considered in this study: as a base
line for appraising change in academic personnel processes in the highly
complex organization known as a research university.

Caplow and McGee had set out on a virgin path "to develop a body of
systematic knowledge about the academic labor market" (*Marketplace*, p.
26). They did, indeed, provide a number of insights into the personnel
processes of research universities, and their work has been cited hun-
dreds of times, and continues to be cited, in spite of the lack of outward
resemblance of the university of 1987 to the university of 1957 in which
they conducted their interviews. As I set out in their footsteps along a
better beaten path, I found what Logan Wilson discovered in 1979: that a
new environment required a new kind of book. And so, this book is not

so much an "Academic Marketplace Revisited" as it is a construction fitting the 1980s, drawing heavily upon the earlier framework, data, and insights.

Clearly the academic world has changed since the 1950s. College and university faculties have encountered and survived the McCarthyism of the 1950s and the student unrest of the 1960s. The Sputnik-fueled expansion of higher education after 1954 exacerbated the postwar situation of a depleted supply of faculty members, but the pendulum swung to a tenured-in, graying faculty and a surplus of taxi-driving Ph.D.'s in the 1970s. The decade of the 1980s began under a cloud of retrenchment following the forced ascendance of the financial manager in the academy; the decade has been further dulled by an adversarial atmosphere that has torn the collegial fabric and contributed to a remarkable growth in campus legal staffs.

We might expect, given the dynamics of the ensuing years, that Caplow and McGee's assessment of academic personnel processes would be hopelessly out of date. They wrote during a period when the demand for college professors had created high mobility among faculty members, when there were typically fewer than ten candidates for a faculty position and often only one, when a department chairman* could "go to a meeting and hire somebody." Today the supply of academic labor is apparently bounteous, there are scores of applicants for a position, and faculty recruitment is affected by organizational constraints of various kinds.

In organizational-behaviorist terms, the university of the 1950s seemed to view faculty members as replaceable parts rather than individual assets—"'He was a theoretical multidimensional geobarbanalyst. They're dirt cheap; we got another.'" (*Marketplace*, p. 102) In this attitude, academia reflected to some degree the scientific management tenets in sway at that time throughout the manufacturing industry, then dominant in the nonacademic sector. In today's post–industrial environment we see a pronounced shift to a service economy, with different behaviors emerging in the nonacademic sector. A telling parallel can be drawn between Walton and Lawrence's (1985) chronological chart of "human resource management systems" in the nonacademic sector and a similar construction for the academic sector (See Table 1). Although American industry and American colleges began their colonial history with widely divergent systems, movement over the decades has brought a surprising convergence.

Today, the corporate world is more *like* the university, and in fact infringes upon the academic world in various forms of education and research. Coupled with this blurring of the distinction between academ-

---

*The term "chairman" is used throughout this study, rather than "chair" or "chairperson," because it was the title used in the majority of the institutions studied.

Table 1:
A Comparison of Nonacademic "American Human Resource Management Systems" with Academic Personnel Systems

	Craft to 1820	Market to WW I	Technical to WW II	Career post-WW II	Commitment (emerging)
Nonacademic	Master/journeyman/ apprentice work team; multiyear mobility from apprentice to journeyman to master; lifetime system.	Unskilled labor in work gangs; high turnover; "Captains of industry."	Fine division of labor; introduction of machines; semi-long-term employment; exempt career barrier; unionization.	Grouping of individual positions under a supervisor; long-term employment; career-oriented; movement up through ranks.	Semi-autonomous work groups; near lifetime employment; slow promotion; lateral and vertical movement.
Academic	Temporary teachers awaiting church appointments; presidents and trustees were often clergymen.	Teaching most important work activity; emerging emphasis on research and specialization; high mobility of faculty; strong presidents; work organized in academic departments; professional associations were founded.		Research professor influential in organization; tenure system increasingly important; high faculty mobility at beginning of period; more selective later.	Semi-autonomous departments; chairmen as managers; slower promotion; expansion of interdisciplinary work; encouraging lateral relationship.

Source: Adapted from Walton and Lawrence (1985); Table 2-1, pp.17-18

ic and nonacademic organizations is the foreign competition for American business that has fostered a "search for excellence" in American firms—a search that identifies an organization's human resources as a primary component of excellence. Has this way of looking at the people of an organization spilled over into the academic arena? We might suspect that it would, especially when we know that the best Ph.D.'s in some fields may be siphoned off into the nonacademic enterprise.

Consequently, this book probes the new academic marketplace to determine whether and where change has occurred. The investigation draws from the Caplow and McGee study and from ensuing research, then focuses on interview data collected during the academic year 1985–86 (described more fully in the appendix). In Chapters 2 through 5 the stars of the study, the faculty respondents, speak. Chapter 2 presents the new academic market as perceived by its participants, with attention given to market characteristics and responding institutional policies—especially noting the research emphasis of the university and aspirations toward higher status (the academic world's "search for excellence"). Chapter 3 deals with the faculty search process, examining the origination and definition of the position, the initial search and screening procedures, and the role of affirmative action in the search. Chapter 4 investigates the selection process, considering the difference between selection procedures and criteria for junior and senior faculty members, the impact of a junior appointment on the department, the circumstances of the offer and acceptance, and certain special cases encountered in the study. Termination is the subject of Chapter 5, on the separation process, addressing dismissal, resignation, retirement, and death. Destinations of dismissed or resigning faculty members and the reasons for and impact of their departures are studied.

Chapter 6 summarizes change (and nonchange) in market and process, and relates the current work to that of Caplow and McGee. Here, too, the nonacademic organization is considered, with comparisons to and implications for academe. Finally, there are considerations for the future.

THE CAPLOW AND MCGEE STUDY AND LATER RESEARCH

The Prestige System

The major finding of the 1958 work was the overriding influence of the prestige system in the academic marketplace—especially the feature of closed and preferential hiring. In fact, candidates were frequently hired without a personal interview, entirely on the basis of secondhand reports, leading to the conclusion that what others thought about a candi-

date might be more important to the recruiting academic department than qualities actually observed in the candidate. Universities recruited within their prestige system, that is, from other universities of like prestige ranking, and a crucial factor for job-seekers was having enough and the right kind of acquaintances to whom their availability could be indicated. Prestige was a threshold qualification, followed by perceived professional compatibility ("fitting in") and after that, other criteria came into play, as evidenced by the oft-quoted recorder response: "He played the recorder. That was the reason we hired him. . . . we thought that would be nice" (*Marketplace*, p. 165).

Prestige also played a part in terminations, appearing as one of the three "motives for migration" and described as a strong lure for academics on the way up (although the majority of moves were downward, motivated by a desire for security or authority).

Therefore, the prestige system could not be underestimated in its effect on the academic market. By virtue of producing the most Ph.D.'s, the major universities controlled the supply of Ph.D.'s, but the supply was differentiated according to the prestige of the sponsor. The candidates from the most prestigious departments with the most prestigious sponsors would end up in the most prestigious departments and so on down the line. Thus, the prestige factor was the major difference between the academic market and the classic labor market: In the academic market, prestige was more important than salary; employers were not interchangeable and employees were not interchangeable.

These theories of doctoral prestige and sponsorship have attracted a considerable amount of attention, through study either of procedure or of placement, and have become thoroughly confirmed in the literature. In fact, even prior to Caplow and McGee's study, Committee B of the American Association of University Professors had published results of a study in 1929 noting that about 73 percent of appointment actions relied to some extent on "acquaintanceship" (being known in the profession) and commenting: "This is so general a policy as to make remark almost unnecessary" (p. 179).

Research after 1958 confirmed the influence of the prestige system in recruitment methods, job placement, and market interaction and by the 1980s the prestige system had become firmly ensconced as a synonym for quality and a primary element of the university social system. (See Table 2 for a summary of selected relevant research.)

The results and implications in the research on disciplinary prestige serve to strengthen Caplow and McGee's basic argument. The research has expanded to include disagreement over ascription versus achievement, a point on which they were mute, and to increase knowledge of the market relationship. The research has extended, in the aggregate, across disciplines, contributing smaller pieces to their big picture ap-

Table 2:
Selected Research on the Prestige System

Date	Researchers	Aspect Studied
1960	Bunnell	Sponsorship in recruiting.
1964	Klugh	Sponsorship in Psychology.
1964	Marshall	Sponsorship in recruiting in chemistry, economics and English departments; prestige as a mobility factor.
1965	Hagstrom	Disciplinary orientation related to deparmental prestige.
1967	Brown	Differentiation by prestige of applicants and hiring institutions; prestige as a mobility factor.
1967	Hargens and Hagstrom	Prestige related to placement in first and later jobs in the physical and biological sciences; interaction of prestige with market.
1967	Marsh and Stafford	Prestige as a mobility factor.
1970	Breneman	Prestige in preparation and placement of Ph.D.'s.
1970	Crane	Prestige related to placement in chemistry, physics, psychology, economics, English, and philosophy.
1971	Lewin and Duchan	Sponsorship in placement of women.
1971	McGee	Prestige as a mobility factor in four-year college.
1972	Love	Observations on prestige system by new Ph.D.
1973	Hargens and Farr	Institutional inbreeding.
1974	Clemente and Sturgis	Prestige related to productivity.
1974	Gross and Grambsch	Prestige related to quality.

6

Date	Researchers	Aspect Studied
1974	Stehr	Prestige related to placement in first and later jobs in sociology.
1975	Solomon and Walters	Prestige in editorial recruitment and article selection for journals.
1977	Dornstein	Prestige as "imperfection" in labor market for professionals and executives.
1979	Long, Allison, and McGinnis	Prestige (including undergraduate) related to placement and to productivity of biochemists.
1979	Reskin	Prestige related to later jobs in the sciences; ascriptive nature of doctoral prestige; interaction of prestige with market.
1979	Wilson	Ascriptive nature of doctoral prestige; interaction of prestige with market.
1980	Smelser and Content	Prestige related to placement and to self-selectiveness of applicants in sociology.
1980	Garvin	Prestige related to economics of the university.
1981	Murray, Rankin, and Magill	Weight of personal contacts in obtaining faculty positions.
1981	Sawyer	Prestige as departmental rather than individual characteristic.
1982	Hargens and Hagstrom	Effect of doctoral prestige in placement in high-consensus and low-consensus disciplines.
1982	Massengale and Sage	Prestige related to placement in first and later jobs in doctorate-granting physical education departments; ascriptive nature of prestige.
1985	Thompson and Zumeta	Prestige related to productivity.

7

proach in the arts and sciences. We can safely acknowledge that doctoral prestige has had a substantial effect on the processes of the academic labor market.

Market Structure

Perhaps the most important external influence on faculty mobility in 1958 was the state of the labor market. Caplow and McGee's data were collected in a seller's market. The market was reflected particularly in the number of early tenure awards, the willingness and ability of assistant professors to move years before the tenure decision, and the small applicant pools for faculty positions. Caplow and McGee found within this larger structure a differentiation in field that again deviated from the classic market structure of interchangeability among employees or employers.

Attention to market structure has provided considerable extension of Caplow and McGee's ideas through a time of change, when the structure had swung from a buyer's market in the 1940s to a seller's market in the 1950s and 1960s, and back to a buyer's market in the 1970s and 1980s. An even more important feature of the academic market, however, is its stratification, causing shortages in the midst of plenty. Academics, by increasing their commitment to the creation of knowledge through research, have become ever more specialized. Consequently, there is no "academic profession;" there are instead clusters of experts, making up a differential market. This differentiation and its effects have been studied in various ways by a number of researchers (see Table 3).

Like Caplow and McGee's findings on the prestige system, their findings and assumptions about market structure have been confirmed by subsequent research. The differentiation they noted (employers were not interchangeable and employees were not interchangeable) has not been disputed. Neither has their contention that most Ph.D.'s are trained in the major universities but only a fraction can be absorbed in the major universities.

Institutional Policies

Like any expanding labor-intensive enterprise, higher education in the 1950s was concerned about a personnel shortage. Institutional policies and practices, however, did not reflect that concern. Caplow and McGee found, for example, a rigid system of budgeting rules whereby a budgeted position became the property of the department, to use as it saw fit. As a result, over the years an assistant professor became a full professor and upon leaving was replaced by a full professor. Although the creation of new budget lines was difficult, there was no mechanism for eliminating obsolete positions. The picture was further complicated

Table 3:
Selected Research on the Academic Market

Date	Researchers	Aspect Studied
1966	Clark	Disciplinary differentiation.
1967	Brown	Constraints and differentiation.
1973	Blau	Institutional, disciplinary, and subfield differentiation.
1973	McGee	College and university similarity.
1973	Shichor	"Trickle-down" effect (placement of candidates from prestigious programs in lower-ranked departments).
1976	Cartter	Utilization of Ph.D.'s
1980	Garvin	Differentiation.
1980	Smelser and Content	Constraints.
1981	Muffo and Robinson	Trickle-down Effect.
1981	Youn	Trickle-down effect; supply and demand effects; differentiation.
1983	Moore and others	Trickle-down effect.
1986	Bowen and Schuster	Utilization of Ph.D.'s; women and minorities as "emergent groups."
1987	Clark	Institutional differentiation.

by the fact that there was no "table of organization" in a university—the job was promoted along with the person. Permitting the staffing needs of the university to be controlled by historical accidents created serious problems in achieving the best utilization of faculty resources in a seller's market.

Another suggested obstacle to optimum utilization of the faculty was the confusion about the academic role that stemmed from uncertainty as to the relative importance of teaching and research. The faculty member's "work assignment" was teaching, but the evaluation of performance was based on research. Indeed, Caplow and McGee made a strong indictment of the research university's emphasis on research: "It is only a slight exaggeration to say that academic success is likely to come to the man who has learned to neglect his assigned duties in order to have more time and energy to pursue his private professional interests" (*Marketplace*, p. 221). The first of their eleven recommendations called for a tenure rank of lecturer to be established for those primarily interested in teaching.

The apparent dichotomy between teaching and research led Caplow and McGee to develop a theory of disciplinary versus institutional attachment as a mobility factor: The more research-oriented faculty member, owing to the identification of research with a discipline rather than an institution, is more likely than the teaching-oriented faculty member to leave the institution. In what may have been an example of "cryptomnesia" (Merton's term for similar ideas arising from independent research at the same time), Gouldner's (1957–58) conclusions about "locals" and "cosmopolitans" in a college setting were concurrently established by Caplow and McGee.

A third institutional policy that contributed to underutilization of human resources was bias in employment. How discrimination on the basis of race, sex, or religion affected academic personnel decisions was mentioned by Committee B in 1929 and, with the addition of political affiliation, by Caplow and McGee in 1958, although it was not given careful study until much later. Caplow and McGee suggested that women were not taken seriously and could not look forward to a normal professional career; similarly, their data indicated that discrimination on the basis of race appeared to be "nearly absolute" (*Marketplace*, p. 226).

The institutional policy emanating from the 1958 study that has received the most attention by researchers in later years is the research-teaching conflict; it has been studied through individual orientation and through institutional reward systems. The later research also includes attention to race and sex bias. (Table 4 summarizes research on institutional policies and practices.)

There is no question that Caplow and McGee's assertions were correct as to the basis of evaluation of a faculty member—it is undoubtedly research. The local-cosmopolitan split also seems to be confirmed, al-

though very recent research may be moving away from a clear-cut division between the two concepts.

As to bias, later research indicates that Caplow and McGee's findings about race and sex bias have been somewhat modified. Nevertheless, bias in the academic marketplace has continued to be viewed by researchers as a problem that has not been solved.

In sum, the Caplow and McGee study and ensuing research show the following: The academic marketplace has been dominated by the prestige system—in recruitment and selection of new faculty members, in the modification of the labor market, and to some extent in other aspects of mobility. Beyond the effect of prestige, the academic labor market has been strongly affected by conditions of differentiation or stratification, by problems of communication, and by a divergence from economic considerations. Bias in the academic marketplace has lessened but has not disappeared.

The alleged conflict between teaching and research has not been resolved. A number of researchers agree with Caplow and McGee's findings and concerns; few offer recommendations or explanations that would reconcile the perceived differences between teaching and research orientations. Finally, a new worry has arisen about the effect of a growing legalism on the university organization.

STUDY CONSIDERATIONS

Taking into account the ensuing research and changed conditions, what can we say about Caplow and McGee's findings in today's context? How have the personnel processes that they examined changed over the decades? Or have they changed at all?

As a point of departure, it may be useful here to recount the eleven recommendations with which Caplow and McGee closed their work (*Marketplace*, pp. 239–255):

1. That the tenure rank of lecturer be established for men primarily interested in teaching.
2. That the order of seniority at each academic level be respected and strengthened, in order to provide institutional rewards to offset those of the academic discipline.
3. That standard base salaries be adopted for all academic ranks, and that salary information be made a matter of public and accessible record.
4. That a standard teaching load, expressed in class hours, be adopted in all departments of the university for all members of the teaching staff.
5. That both the period of probationary appointments and the period of probation be much extended, to correct the condition of award of tenure before a reputation is established.

Table 4:
Selected Research on Policies and Practices

Date	Researchers	Aspect Studied
1957-58	Gouldner	Locals and cosmopolitans (research/teaching typology of institutional versus disciplinary identification).
1964	Bernard	Sex bias in prestige system.
1967	Simon, Clark, and Galway	Sex related to productivity.
1971	Lewin and Duchan	Sex bias in placement.
1972	Rafky	Market constraints related to black academicians.
1973	Abrahamson	Functional effects on faculty salaries.
1973	Blau	Loyalty to institution.
1974	Blau	Mobility motivators.
1974	Flango and Brumbaugh	Locals and cosmopolitans.
1974	Mommsen	Employment patterns of black academicians.
1975	Lewis	Merit versus ascription.
1975	Trow and Fulton	Publishing activity; salary effects.
1977	Moore and Newman	Sex bias in placement.
1979	Marwell, Rosenfeld, and Spilerman	Constraints of marriage on academic women.

12

Date	Researchers	Aspect Studied
1980	Smelser and Content	Political and bureaucratic dimensions; search procedures.
1982	Massengale and Sage	Professionalism; sex bias in placement.
1983	Menges and Exum	"Worth" versus "merit" in placement of female and minority academicians.
1984	Baker and Zey-Ferrell	Locals and cosmopolitans.
1984	Kasten	Research activity related to reward system.
1984	Sacco and Milana	Research emphasis.
1984	VanMaanen and Barley	Professionalism.
1985	Alpert	Matrix relationships of discipline and institution; research orientation.
1986	Dill	Organizational culture.
1986	Kaplowitz	Recruiting practices.
1987	Carson and Navarro	Recruiting practices in economics departments.

13

6. That the fringe benefits of faculty employment be improved and expanded.

7. That the personal and arbitrary control of administrative officers over members of the faculty be reduced as far as possible.

8. That existing procedures for the location of candidates to fill vacant faculty positions be improved by increasing the amount of available information.

9. That regular, orderly procedures be established for the selection of a new faculty member from a roster of candidates.

10. That regular, orderly procedures be established for promotion and for the renewal of contracts.

11. That the existence of a faculty vacancy be established always on the basis of demonstrated need for a particular position, and never on the basis of automatic succession.

Which of these recommendations have been realized? Which are still appropriate? Which have become moot?

In pursuit of answers to these questions, I examined the present academic marketplace in the same way and in the same institutions that it was investigated by Caplow and McGee in 1958. My reenactment of the Caplow and McGee study took place in an environment of concern about enrollment trends, government support, and other negative signals in the higher education community. Looking beyond the present, however, one sees the retirement trends and the enormous faculty needs of the 1990s—which have been estimated at 500,000 new faculty members over the next twenty-five years—necessitating an understanding and perhaps improvement of the process by which the faculty perpetuates itself. The real value of the current study, therefore, lies in the future.

2

The New Academic Market

> Things are really *fluky* in the academic world. One can't get
> too caught up in the whole thing. Prestige etcetera are 80
> percent an artifact of advancing age. People don't understand
> how everything is kind of conditioned by the overall market
> in higher education. It has little to do with our own merit or
> efforts.
>
> ASSOCIATE PROFESSOR OF HISTORY

The environment of higher education has changed dramatically since
the late 1950s. Then, the increasingly differentiated academic market
was expanding at an unprecedented rate, and demand for Ph.D.'s was
high; furthermore, the participants in the market were overwhelmingly
white and male. Now, higher education has experienced a period of
retrenchment and stabilization characterized by a low demand for
Ph.D.'s; at the same time that the market was shrinking, the population
of participants was expanding to include women and minorities. Then,
institutional policies were generally unresponsive to market needs: Budgeting rules were rigid and restrictive, discouraging flexibility in staffing. Now, the marketplace shows adaptive behavior in new forms of
management that have increased flexibility, especially to serve an institutional quest for higher status.

Then, a growing emphasis on research was changing the nature of the
marketplace; now, the research emphasis is well entrenched as an agent
of differentiation between types of institutions. There is no monolithic
"higher education," but rather a scaling of institutions, with proprietary
schools and community colleges at one end of the spectrum and prestigious research universities at the other, with the midpoints occupied
by comprehensive universities, selective liberal arts colleges, etc. There
is further differentiation among and within academic disciplines—as
between, for example, English and economics, or American history and
Southeast Asian history.

And in spite of environmental pressures, the academic market remains separate, similar to but distinguished from the nonacademic
world. Although features such as a search for excellence and other re-

sponses to external forces align academic with nonacademic organizations, the market has unique characteristics that maintain separation.

UNIQUE CHARACTERISTICS

Caplow and McGee, followed by Smelser and Content (1980), remarked
on the unique supply and demand nature of the academic labor market,
with a set of universities both producing Ph.D.'s and creating the demand for them. Nowhere in this study did the dual role of the faculty
member in the academic labor market—recruiting for the demand and
responsibility for placement of the supply—emerge so strongly as in
discussions about the market itself. In a majority of cases, responsibility
for placing graduate students was predominant in the chairman's attitude; an increase in job opportunities was expressed in positive terms,
even though it would make recruiting more difficult, and a lack of increase was viewed negatively.

Views from both sides of the job fence were similar. For example,
chairmen and new appointees said essentially the same things—as
these comments from a chairman of physics and from a new assistant
professor of physics at different schools illustrate:

The market is much better; there are plenty of ads.

The market has changed for the better, from no jobs to quite a few jobs.

Or, in a more discriminating response from a chairman of a large economics department and from a new assistant professor in a small language department, in different schools:

My impression is that there are dual job markets in economics. The elite institutions are falling all over themselves trying to get a very small group of talented
people, and then there is the rest of the world. For the best people, the sky is the
limit!

Different generalizations can be made for different levels of candidate. For example, people from the best schools, people from the middle schools, people from
the poorest schools, the best students from the best schools, the best students
from the middle schools, etc. The market will affect all those groups differently.

In apparent empathy with his graduate students, one chairman of
classics said, almost gleefully:

The market has improved and I think it will continue. I foresee days when we'll
be right back where we were in the '60s and I'll be pulling people off the street.

Confirming Bowen and Schuster's (1986) findings about perceived
improvement of the market, more than half of the responding chairmen

considered the academic labor market to be improved and improving for placement of Ph.D.'s: 48 percent of the humanities chairmen; 53 percent of the natural sciences chairmen; and most optimistic, the social sciences chairmen at 71 percent. In today's buyer's market, there is a guardedly optimistic air, a general feeling across disciplinary divisions that demand for Ph.D.'s may be on the upswing.

Differentiation of the market within disciplines plays a role, however, so that in a disciplinary market viewed as good, one or more subfields may be less promising, or in a discipline where the market is viewed as bad or not improving, a subfield may be otherwise. Clinical and developmental psychology were seen as thriving fields in an otherwise stable market in psychology; nuclear physics was considered on the decline within a good physics market. In an anthropology market generally viewed as bad, one new appointee said (and her opinion was verified by other anthropologists):

There is a real future for anthropologists interested in nutrition, population, health in developing countries. This is my specialty and I think its future has just begun.

Further differentiation of demand in the academic labor market was believed to be caused indirectly by the external environment. For example, international trade was reflected in language study: Chinese and Japanese were viewed as growing areas, Arabic declining; interest has been piqued in Italian:

Italian studies have improved considerably in the past ten years. There is a recognition that Italian is valuable in personal improvement; Italian trade and fashion contacts have expanded enormously and there is a much greater awareness of Italy's importance. Italian Americans are more willing to go to their roots versus the assimilation that earlier immigrants tried to achieve.

Political interest in Latin America has apparently contributed to a healthy market in Spanish and Portugese. The market for linguistics has improved, with a shift toward applied linguistics (e.g., English as a foreign language).

A more direct influence was evidenced by several physicists who noted that the future of high energy physics was dependent upon the political fate of the Superconducting Super Collider. And the impact of federal policy was also observed in nonscientific fields, as witness this remark by a professor of Arabic studies:

The job market in Arabic studies is very much prey to national priorities set in NDEA—any decision to increase resources needs Title XI funding. Fluctuation to better is a national matter (although fluctuation to worse can be a local decision). Arabic became more important and more popular as a result of the in-

creasing importance of the Middle East in the 1970s. This has crested and probably won't increase.

The differentiation of supply, too, was seen as specifically affected by national priorities in education, as manifested in federal funding of training grants, graduate scholarships, postdoctoral funds, etc. Declines and inclines in federal support were seen as causing fluctuation in Ph.D. production among disciplines, although note these comments from the humanities:

I am surprised that the field has continued to flourish without the kind of full fellowship support that I had. Our students are working part-time and doing without that kind of financial assistance.

This is a very positive department, but we would all be happier if we had more money for graduate students.

Future shortages in supply were pinpointed in another approach to differentiation, as by this assistant professor of geography:

We are not producing very many people in some specialties, and the people in those specialties will have their pick of the jobs in the 1990s. I would advise students to go into things not highly practical at the moment, like area, regional specialization. Now we are hiring one to three a year in the field, but we will need a lot more.

In similarly upbeat terms, an assistant professor talked about the currently thriving field of computer science:

I don't expect things to change much. Demand is surely going to stay there. Demand for the lower level computer science degree may not be sustained, but at the Master's and Ph.D. level I see no end to the demand. Ground level programming people are being replaced by more sophisticated systems, but there will never be an end to the demand for people who can solve the more complex problems.

Another cause of differentiation, the important external factor of non-academic competition for new Ph.D.'s, was described in a number of fields such as economics, telecommunications, biology, computer science, chemistry, and physics. A biologist spoke in these terms:

In molecular biology the market has changed very dramatically. Industrial jobs in biotechnology have changed it completely. I suspect that research support may be better in industry. You can actually do postdocs in industry if you choose.

In addition, alluding to competition from professional schools (for arts and sciences faculty), an economist remarked:

One of the main developments over the last few years has been a growth in business schools. So that means a lot of $50,000 jobs out there in business schools for us. A lot of very fine people are going into business schools now. There is not the stigma attached to it that there once was.

Nonacademic opportunities for Ph.D.'s have improved for less likely disciplines as well. Here is a response from a chairman of anthropology:

Ten to fifteen years ago all of our Ph.D.'s would get jobs in academia. Now only 10 to 20 percent get academic jobs. They work as research organizers, with computers in business and industry, and in contract archaeology.

A general attitude toward nonacademic employment was typified by this comment:

There is a nonacademic market and more people are willing to consider non-academic jobs now than previously—it has become "socially acceptable."

Beyond the external influences, the market could be affected by an internal change in a field as well. Internally generated change was cited by this new appointee, a professor of immunology:

The market is better now than it was five years ago. There are ten academic positions now open across the country. Partially this is cancer research but also the advent of biomedicine, better defined. We can now identify the important molecules, whereas it was a highly intuitive science previously.

A bulge of retirements—another internal influence—will affect the market in the very near future. Retirements in this sample were projected, through an aggregation of data from chairmen, at an average of 15 percent of the faculty retiring by 1995 (based on a total of 495 expected retirements in this sample of 3,302 faculty members). Only slight variances occurred by type of institution (16 percent public, 14 percent private) and by disciplinary division (17 percent humanities, 13 percent social sciences, 15 percent natural sciences). Differences did occur by discipline (7 percent in economics, 24 percent in physics) but the data became small samples at that level and were therefore less reliable; departmental differences might have been distorted, for example, by the effect of subfields such as econometrics, which is a "young" field. Another comparison may be made by department ranking, where the retirement rate was projected as higher than average, 20 percent, in the departments ranked below the top twenty, and 14 percent for departments among the top twenty—thus providing an apparent opportunity for upgrading through judicious staffing in the lower-ranked departments.

The degree of staffing preparation for these expected retirements var-

ied among institutions and particularly among departments and divisions within institutions, with some displaying long-range planning skills, others mired in short-term thinking, and an ad hoc attitude in between. The first approach is described in this comment from a chairman in a large state school:

The dean came up with a special program for hiring in our department. Because we have too many people in a certain age group, instead of replacing retirees, the hiring is going on at a steady rate. We have been hiring about one and a half people a year in anticipation of retirements.

The in-between method is used at the state university where this chairman said:

In this department we will have a recruiting job that will be unprecedented and it will be even worse in some other departments. The university lets the departments borrow appointments against anticipated retirements, but it is a matter of negotiation, not policy.

And in spite of the specific knowledge about coming retirements on a particular campus, as well as general knowledge of increasing retirements throughout higher education, this response from a chairman at the third state university in the sample was not atypical:

We have a number of people retiring and it is going to be a problem for us. I have tried to tell the dean that we should be thinking about this now. Our dean would welcome a policy of replacing them three or four years hence!

A counter-influence that was expected by some respondents to have an impact on the academic labor market was the number of Ph.D.'s who had trickled down to less research-oriented schools because of lack of choice when they entered the job market. Although a number of graduates of top programs self-selected to liberal arts colleges, they thought others would prefer to be in a department with an active and stimulating research program. Additionally, several chairmen noted that although the quantity of openings was increasing, the applicant pool was inflated by "itinerant scholars" (people who had not been successful in finding permanent positions), as well as by the assistant professors who were trying to be upwardly mobile. At least part of this soft market of nontraditional candidates may, however, be influenced by the development of research programs in schools formerly less research-oriented—the academic grapevine buzzes with news of research being "beefed up" in numerous places.

The dynamism of the market is reflected in this comment from a professor of chemistry:

Up until three years ago my field, theoretical chemistry, had been static for about ten years. In a very short period six or seven senior people moved; there was a lot of action at the mature but young full professor stage. Then if one person moves, it creates a "hole." There are good young people, too—a pool of capable graduate students. Good students from a good university can call their shots in chemistry.

A few respondents viewed the market as a secondary concern. Confirming Caplow and McGee's and others' belief in the unique quality of the academic marketplace, one assistant professor commented:

My perception of myself in relation to other people doing history colors my feeling about the job market. I went into school thinking that I would get a Ph.D. for the intrinsic value, not for the job *per se*, and I may have been lucky. But getting an assistant professorship is like getting a big part in a play—maybe you'll be a star some day, maybe not.

And a chairman said:

The job market is mercurial, feast or famine. It is high risk, like the Foreign Legion. You get into it because you can't think of anything else you want to spend your life doing.

RESEARCH CULTURE

The unique quality of academia may foster a commitment that is related to another force of differentiation, this between types of institutions in the academic labor market: the research emphasis, both of the research university (demand) and of the Ph.D.'s it produces (supply). Caplow and McGee recognized the increasing emphasis on research in the university in 1958; this study extended their understanding of transition to a well entrenched reality. In fact, as Dill (1986) has pointed out, research typifies the organizational culture of the contemporary research university. Indeed, the idea of research is seen by some, including this chairman, as driving the university: "The university is a place where you ought to be able to invest in long-range research."

Extension of the research investment is found in many universities that have separate research organizations, as described by this chairman:

The research organizations are administratively separate from the university. Their sources of funding are separate and their appointments are without academic tenure. There is a good deal more freedom in the kind of research that can be done than in industry. It is not uncommon to have joint appointments between the research organization and the department. Neither is it uncommon

for someone to take a leave to work full time in the research organization. The research organization has what is called "industrial associates" who are invited to participate in various research projects through a prospectus; they have no control over the research.

The notion of a research culture is amply supported in this study by persons making hiring decisions and those accepting positions. Qualifications for positions were expressed by chairmen in terms of research interests:

The most important qualification is scholarly promise as evidenced in written work (how much, where, what quality).

The person should have his or her own strong research specialty, but we look for someone who will contribute to the interdisciplinary work in the department.

We wanted someone who had made a significant contribution to the field in quantitative methods.

I must admit that research is the most important factor.

And new assistant professors echoed the qualification emphasis in their reasons for accepting the job offer:

The overriding factor was the strength of the integrated research effort in this department—volume and quality—the general reputation the place has for research in chemistry, both in industry and academia. That is the one and only factor.

I was attracted by the quality of the faculty in general, the research facilities, and a number of people not only in the history department with interests similar to mine.

We were attracted, number one, by a department big enough for the potential for us to work together and, number two, by the quality of the program. We wanted Ph.D. students, other research faculty, and research facilities.

I made a decision at a certain point that I was more interested in being in a research-oriented university than in a teaching-oriented college. I made that decision gradually. My original desire to go into academics developed in high school when my father was a mature graduate student at Berkeley. Then we moved to a small school in Virginia and I liked the setting, I liked the idea of sitting around reading books. But I was fortunate enough to select a dissertation topic that opened up all sorts of research possibilities to me. I guess the critical moment came when I was asked during a job interview which kind of school I preferred; I realized that I preferred the research university.

The importance of these shared values should not be underestimated. Although faculty members view themselves as teachers, they also acknowledge the primacy of the research—that is, analysis of existing

knowledge and creation of new knowledge—that drives the teaching. The conditions differ markedly from the earlier study. Caplow and McGee made a major point of the conflict between teaching and research in the personnel process, recommending (their Recommendation No. 1) that a tenure rank of lecturer be established for those not interested in research; we find their recommendation repeated in the Carnegie report on undergraduate education (Boyer 1987). This study finds that recommendation largely irrelevant in a research university. There appears to be substantial agreement between hiring departments and job candidates that the candidate is being hired to do research and will be evaluated on the basis of his or her research. Opportunities for research play a major role in the candidates' career decisions—suggesting that any behavioral change in the balance of teaching and research, were it desirable, would have to originate in graduate education, before the Ph.D. becomes a faculty member.

The downside of this research emphasis came from a private university, where research funding might be more important, in a comment from an associate professor of economics:

The undergraduates here are getting short-changed and they know it, we know it, the administration knows it. We all know it. If you want an education, go to a four-year liberal arts college.

Such a minority (in this research university sample) position aside, the argument that an assistant professor is hired to teach and is evaluated on research does not prevail in the contemporary research university. Derek Bok clarified the nonargument in *Higher Learning* (1986):

There is an implication that professors are selfish and intent only on enhancing their scholarly reputations, with little acknowledgement of the intense effort required to serve simultaneously as undergraduate teachers, mentors of graduate students, and scholars seeking to enlarge knowledge and understanding. In stressing the virtues of effective pedagogy, moreover, critics often fail to recognize the immense importance of research, not just in contributing to the general store of knowledge but in helping to sustain the vitality of professors by ensuring that they continue to have something of genuine importance to teach. (pp. 64–65)

Bok's reference to effort is echoed in the conscientious character of this report from a newly appointed full professor who came to the university from a research organization:

Last semester I spent 90 percent of my time on teaching, including getting some graduate research established. This semester it's a little less; I'm trying for sixty-forty. Of course the "clock" is built around classes and teaching, the day-to-day involvement with students, the development of teacher-student relationships. I

am trying to mix my priorities and get things balanced. I try to emphasize research one semester and teaching the other.

A more difficult question may be the effect of a research orientation on the faculty member's relationship to the department or institution. Based upon a pronounced duality that may no longer exist, Caplow and McGee developed (concomitant with Gouldner, 1957–58) a theory of a disciplinary attachment associated with research versus an institutional attachment associated with teaching. The faculty member with a research orientation was considered to be more strongly attached to the discipline and more likely to leave the institution. Are the earlier findings relevant in the new academic market? Well, yes and no, as indicated in Figure 1.

The data from this study concerning disciplinary or institutional orientation were aggregated according to rank and mobility status: assistant professors who were dismissed, assistant professors who resigned, associate and full professors who resigned, members of any rank who retired. As might be expected, there was a considerable difference between the profiles of the assistant professors who were dismissed and those who resigned, with 47 percent of the former and 73 percent of the latter well known in the discipline outside the institution. Only about a third of the assistant professors (35 percent for the combined group—no difference between dismissals and resignations) were well known in the institution. At the senior level, there was little difference in the percentage of persons who had both strong institutional ties and strong disciplinary ties—74 percent for retirees and 75 percent for associate professors and professors who resigned. The retirees had stronger ties with the institution (87 percent versus 80 percent, perhaps owing to their seniority) and those who had resigned had stronger disciplinary ties (95 percent versus 82 percent). But notice that these data suggest a strong discipline-oriented approach at the stage of building a career, with institutional orientation becoming more important as a career advances. (See corroboration of this idea in Dressel et al. 1970 and Baldwin and Blackburn 1981.) The career cycle may match a life cycle, which could partially account for the lack of mobility at the associate professor rank, as indicated in this comment:

There is a bit more local identification at the associate professor rank. People have kids in the schools, have houses, are involved in the community, etc.

It is possible, too, that if research is indeed integral to the culture of the institution, a research orientation in itself may no longer pull the faculty member away from the institution. As indicated by this study, it was lack of *particular* research compatibility that pushed the faculty members in the sample toward new jobs and *particular* research oppor-

Figure 1
Disciplinary/Institutional Orientation of the Departing Faculty Member, by
Rank and Type of Termination

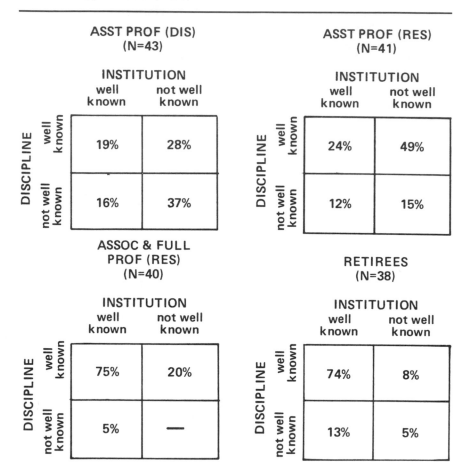

tunities that attracted them, not a difference between a teaching and a
research orientation, as shown in this comment about an associate professor's departure: "He went to Illinois; he has more compatible colleagues for his area of research there." The local-cosmopolitan argument
may be too general and simplistic for application to faculty mobility in
the new academic market.

Another element that illuminates the effect of a research orientation is
collaboration with colleagues. Caplow and McGee investigated incidence of collaboration within the department in an attempt to determine
whether it carried any weight in a faculty member's decision to leave,

and concluded that it did not. Identical results were obtained in the current study. Considering those faculty members who had left the department (124 terminations), about a third had collaborated in research with members of the department. Excluding the humanities, where collaboration in research and publication was rare (only four cases reported), the breakdown of the remaining eighty-four cases showed no effect on mobility: Exactly half of the sample (forty-two) had collaborated with colleagues and half had not done so. There was virtually a fifty-fifty split at all ranks and little difference between disciplinary divisions in intradepartmental collaboration.

Not indicated in those numbers, though, was another type of collaboration—that which took place with members of other departments or other institutions. Often interinstitutional collaboration resulted from professional ties established before the faculty member had joined the department. Frequently intrainstitutional collaboration grew out of contacts established through interdisciplinary programs. In some instances, collaboration was taking place between the faculty member who had left and someone still in the department. Collaboration therefore appears as a complicated factor, crossing organizational boundaries and exerting a complex influence as part of the research orientation.

The complexity included a formalized system of collaboration, interdisciplinary (or multidisciplinary) research, which occurred on all of the campuses in the sample. The opportunity to participate in interdisciplinary research was a plus in recruitment, especially for the new assistant professor, as shown in these comments:

I'm in language linguistics and this department has a pretty well developed language linguistics division. I'm an interdisciplinary person and this is a better place for some interesting and stimulating contact.

I was attracted by the department's reputation—its openness to interdisciplinary research. I have degrees in two social science disciplines and pursue research in both.

This department is uniquely connected with other departments. The interdisciplinary opportunities are very important to me.

Interest in opportunities for interdisciplinary work crossed divisional lines, as these chairmen indicated:

Art History: We are very liberal on interdisciplinary work. This university has number one departments in related fields—history, English—and this is important as the field becomes more interdisciplinary. We have incredible depth here. Actually, the departmental structure is becoming obsolete.

Religious Studies: This field is interdisciplinary in nature. I personally hope that the interface between computers and textual analysis opens up in religious studies. This university supports interdisciplinary efforts; they like to have peo-

ple who work in more than one department, so that the interdisciplinary effort is supported.

History: The Latin American studies program allows interaction with other disciplines. It's best not to have one's life concentrated in the department. That way the department doesn't get all the stress.

Physiology: There is an idea afloat that the structure of biology is changing and that the old disciplines don't have much meaning anymore. A lot of people feel their discipline is getting obsolete, not only in the sciences. Graduate students are not attracted to a name like 'botany.' We are trying to organize around research interests.

QUEST FOR QUALITY

The research culture, depending as it does upon reputation in the academic discipline, places the research university in a competitive arena where comparative advantage in recruiting is crucial to success. This comparative advantage often emanates from "image," derived from the prestige accepted in academia as a measure of quality. Prestige "conveys ideas of leadership, of power, and, above all, of excellence" (Gross and Grambsch 1974, p. 100); it is the characteristic by which faculty, students, and research grants are attracted. Consequently, prestige is an essential ingredient of the university social system, and further, academic departments are seen as prestige-maximizing units (Garvin 1980) through the professional reputations of individual department members.

So it comes as no surprise that a number of prestige-building efforts in staffing were described by respondents in this study. A prevalent attraction was a well-respected center or institute that would accommodate the research needs of a prospective faculty member; another device was the creation of special prestigious chairs that were university rather than departmental appointments. But by far the most heavily used technique was simply the faculty appointment within the department.

Therein lay some disagreement. Responding chairmen expressed different philosophies for strengthening a department. Some believed in change at the top and some believed in building from the bottom; the difference in opinion seemed to be influenced by the current ranking of the chairman's department. For example, the chairman of a department ranked below the top ten asserted:

If you really want to build a department, you have to bring in senior people from outside and pay them well.

By contrast, examples from chairmen of two top-ranked departments favored the bottom-up theory:

Our improved quality has come about through luck and prayer! We haven't brought in a senior star for twenty years.

I was a partisan for senior appointments, but we have had such good luck in these two junior appointments that I am now against the senior searches.

There was mention of the growth and development of Ph.D. programs and a general increase in "standards." Rankings were important; every chairman in a rated discipline knew where his or her department stood in the latest published rankings. There were several comments about aspiring to "move up" in the rankings, aiming for the "top ten," etc., using staffing as a vehicle for movement. The increasingly competitive environment of higher education has resulted in a quest for higher ratings that was not present thirty years ago.

These aspirations may be placed in a certain perspective by looking at the top ten departments in three disciplines (those that were represented in the study sample in all six schools) in the Roose and Andersen (1970) and Jones et al. (1982) ratings:

	1970	1982
English:	Yale	Yale
	Harvard	Berkeley
	Berkeley	Virginia
	Chicago	Harvard
	Princeton	Chicago
	Columbia	Columbia
	Stanford	Cornell
	Johns Hopkins	Johns Hopkins
	Cornell	Princeton
	Virginia	Stanford
Economics:	Harvard	MIT
	MIT	Harvard
	Chicago	Chicago
	Yale	Stanford
	Berkeley	Princeton
	Princeton	Yale
	Michigan	Minnesota
	Minnesota	Pennsylvania
	Pennsylvania	Columbia
	Stanford	Berkeley
Physics:	Berkeley	Cal Tech
	Cal Tech	Harvard
	Harvard	Berkeley
	Princeton	Princeton
	MIT	MIT
	Stanford	Cornell
	Columbia	Chicago

	1970	1982
Physics:	Illinois	Stanford
	Chicago	Columbia
	Cornell	Illinois

Although there was some jockeying for position within the elite group, there was little change over a decade. Given this continuity of ranking and the cynicism it may engender in lower-ranked departments, it was not surprising to find the study revealing human fallout from the search for excellence, as typified by this senior faculty member's remark:

I have an iron in the fire and I hope it burns. I will leave here if I can. There is a general feeling of being unappreciated.

PARTICIPANTS IN THE MARKET

Concurrent with the change to a pronounced research orientation and aspirations to greater prestige, changes have occurred in the labor market. In terms of quantity, the majority of the chairmen indicated an increase in the number of applicants for a junior position. Sixty-seven percent of the chairmen said that there were more candidates for positions today; more than half of the 17 percent who thought otherwise were in the natural sciences. (Sixteen percent of the respondents were not sure whether there had been an increase or decrease.) Among the majority, there were reservations as to field, reflecting the differentiation noted earlier.

As to the quality found in the larger applicant pools, decline was not a major concern. Thirty-five percent of the chairmen thought that today's candidates were *better* than those of twenty years ago:

I think better students are going into economics. There is a greater emphasis on developing good scholarship earlier in the training. It is not unusual for our assistant professor candidates to have published papers in major journals. When I was on the job market, it was easy to get a job and we were sort of encouraged to be lazy.

I think we do have better candidates. They are superb. But then the department gets better and attracts better people and there is a cyclical action to that.

People in graduate school are very good, highly motivated.

Many of the chairmen pointed out the *difference* in training as opposed to quality:

It's hard to put "better" into perspective because there are a lot more things to be trained in and as chemists they know more because there is more to be

known. The science has progressed. Whether they are trained better, I don't really think so.

Whether they're better is a subject of an awful lot of dispute. I would say that the younger faculty members that we see in political science, I would consider yes, they are very well trained in things on the frontier, but no, they tend to be quite often from my perspective narrow technicians. They have marketable skills but things get lost in the process.

Beyond the total numbers and general quality, an area of difference projected for the supply side of the market was a greater diversity in the participants. Whereas Caplow and McGee identified bias as a determinant in the academic labor market that excluded persons on the basis of sex, religion, race, and political affiliation, today's marketplace is theoretically open to all. Religion and political affiliation do not appear to be a factor in research university employment; substantially more women and minorities are seen in today's market and the prognosis for women seems quite good. A chairman of chemistry said:

A big change in the job market will be the number of women teaching. Our graduate enrollment is up and has reached a critical mass; availability will be about 40 percent in a few years.

A change in the representation of women and minorities could already be seen in the breakdown of appointments (see Table 5). In the current study, women constituted slightly less than a third of the appointments at the junior level, slightly more than a fifth at the senior level, and 28 percent of the total. Minorities were 7 percent of the total. The Caplow and McGee sample of ninety-one appointments included only four women, an instructor in speech and drama and two instructors and an associate professor in home economics, and one Asian associate professor in mathematics.

The change in the participation rate of women is reflected in the workforce statistics as well. Of the 795 assistant professors among the 3,302 faculty members of the departments studied, 218, or 27 percent, were women. (Unfortunately, comparable statistics for the 1958 faculty are not available; but the exclusive use of the nouns "man" and "men" by Caplow and McGee in referring to faculty members attests to the scarcity of females.)

A derivative of the entry of women into professional employment in larger numbers is a major concern expressed by the respondents in this study: The new academic market is perceptibly affected by the spouse employment issue. In this sample it was a factor in almost 20 percent of the resignations and appointments. The group of appointments included two academic couples (a professor, an assistant professor, and two associate professors), each in the same department, and the resigna-

Table 5:
Breakdown of Appointments, by Race and Sex

| | Number of Appointments | | | | |
| | | White | | Minority | |
Study/Rank	Total	Male	Female	Male	Female
1958					
Instructor or					
Assistant Professor	66	63	3	--	--
Associate and					
Full Professor	25	23	1	1 Asian	--
Total	91	86	4	1	--
1986					
Assistant Professor	96	62	26	1 Black	1 Hisp
				3 Asian	3 Asian
Associate and					
Full Professor	41	31	9	1 Black	--
Total	137	93	35	5	4

tions included one academic couple (two assistant professors) from the same department. Excluding those six people, a breakdown by rank and sex of the departing or appointed faculty members is shown in Table 6. As a proportion of total female appointments, 18 percent of the women were affected by spouse employment problems; 19 percent of the men appointed were affected. Similarly, 21 percent of the departing women and 19 percent of the departing men were affected.

Spouses needing employment may be part of an academic couple or seeking nonacademic jobs, but their needs are a visible and demanding variable in the faculty personnel picture. Unlike the Marwell et al. (1979) conclusions based on 1970 data, mobility constraints imposed by marriage were seen to affect men and women equally in this study. A difference in the sample in this study, of course, is the newly appointed or departing faculty member of either sex, with a professionally but not necessarily academically employed spouse, as compared to the academic men and women in place in the Marwell study. Nevertheless, the time lapse of a decade and a half between the Marwell data base and this one more likely provides the heavier weight.

In addition to specific resignations and appointments in this sample, there were other recent incidents recounted by respondents. Several chairmen offered accounts of losing women from their offer or short lists

Table 6:
Spouse Employment Effect on Mobility

Type of Action/Rank	Number of Faculty Members Affected		
	Total	Male	Female
Resignations			
Assistant Professor	7	5	2
Associate Professor	5	4	1
Professor	4	4	-
Total Affected	16	13	3
Total Resignations	81	67	14
Appointment			
Assistant Professor	15	10	5
Associate Professor	5	3	2
Professor	6	6	-
Total Affected	26	19	7
Total Appointments	137	98	39

in the past two years because their husbands could not find jobs; this was a typical comment:

We were looking for a senior person in Baroque, and we recruited basically through contacting people that we knew. The top candidate was a woman from Texas who wanted to come, but we were not able to find a job for her husband and they both ended up going to Michigan.

Other chairmen reported similar difficulties with senior men whose wives could not relocate satisfactorily, as in this case:

Our first offer was to a Bell Labs person whose wife would not move. She had just been promoted to a job in which she was very happy.

The problems of spouse employment were articulated carefully by some respondents, as typified in these two comments:

Spouse employment raises very serious questions of equity, expediency. It is rare that you find two equally qualified people, and at a prestigious institution, if you hire both, you usually make a decision to lower your standards in some form or other, or you have a second group of faculty who are dependents, or you are simply spending a lot of money.

There are two significant problems in spouse employment: If the two people are very much alike in their academic pursuits or if one is of obviously higher quality.

A chairman and a peer respondent were members of commuting couples—a commuting distance of about two hundred miles. One chairman
had very recently received an offer from another university but had
rejected it because his wife was happy in her academic job and the
recruiting university had hedged on the subject of a position for her.

It was generally conceded that spouse employment was a critical factor in the academic marketplace, as reflected in these comments:

The spouse problems are terrible these days. It's a factor in two-thirds of our
offers. We are always calling the Medical School and they are calling us trying to
work out arrangements.

The spouse problem has become the most important problem in faculty recruiting. I have tried to organize a consortium in this area for spouse hiring.

On the other hand, there was (as always) the minority conservative
viewpoint:

Spouse employment is a variable of individuals. I would not make a position for
anyone, although we lost a woman from Arizona whose husband needed a job.

Several new appointees made comments about spouse employment,
characterized by these quotes:

My wife has an M.A. in English (ABD) and she got a job at the Press, but she
looked for about ten months when we first came and was getting pretty
discouraged.

Spouse employment is *the* big problem in recruiting. If it weren't for the fact that
my wife hates big cities, we would be moving now that she has her MBA. As it
is, she is doing entrepreneurial things here and enjoying it.

When I got this job my husband was at Toronto in economics and the department here invited him as a visitor, with the understanding that he would go into
a tenure track position the following year. They changed their mind about the
tenure track position and he went back to Toronto. Then they offered him a
probationary tenure track slot. He is currently in Berkeley on a national fellowship, and it looks as though we both may be on the job market next year.

And an historical perspective was offered by some older faculty
members:

My wife is a faculty member in another department here and it was important to
us when I was looking for a job that she find one as well. People just didn't talk
about it in those days.

When I came to this department, there was a superb geneticist here. She was
quite good, but her husband was also a geneticist and he was a professor. She

was on a one-year appointment as a lecturer. She scrounged around for money
to do her research and he had the best of all possible worlds. My wife had a
Ph.D. but we never considered looking for a job for her when I came here. She
stayed home with the family for some years and then went back to doing odd job
things. That has all changed.

INSTITUTIONAL RESPONSES

Unlike the 1950s, in the 1980s we find many and varied management
strategies that respond to the new academic market. Perhaps the most
prominent change relates to Caplow and McGee's complaint of rigid
budgeting rules that froze positions in place. A new flexibility in resource allocation has encouraged two phenomena found in the current
study: central funds made available to departments for special hiring;
and shifting of positions from rank and department.

At three of the schools studied, there was a "target of opportunity"
recruiting arrangement that covered special appointments of all kinds,
including prestigious senior candidates. At another institution, the
funding specifically applied only to women and minorities. At another,
there was only a "superstar" fund, but additional money could be provided for campus interviews of women and minorities.

None of these arrangements was particularly effective. The history of
various programs since their inception showed participation by only
nineteen of the departments in the sample; all but one of the participating departments were in the humanities or social sciences, thirteen were
in private universities. The use varied: six departments (all in private
schools) had appointed senior white males; three departments in private
schools and three in public universities had appointed women; four
departments in a single private university had appointed blacks. In the
public university where candidate visits were underwritten, three departments had used the funds. All of the departments represented in
the study that in the past had hired or interviewed women and minority
candidates through special programs were ranked in the top twelve,
with six in the top five.

Perhaps the "target of opportunity" procedure has proved ineffective
because it is not a clearly defined position given to the specific department—as is, say, an assistant professor position in a physics department—and as such carries uncertainty about the future effect on the
department of using the special funds to add a person now. There seems
to be sufficient vagueness attached to that kind of budget incentive to
result in its use primarily by the presumably more confident and aggressive top-ranked departments.

The second example of flexibility addresses Caplow and McGee's as-
sertion that a department was permitted to "own" a position, such that a
full professor vacancy would automatically be filled by a full professor in

the same department. In this study, there was considerable administrative control over faculty positions at the outset, that is, at the point of the authorization to recruit, if not in the intellectual decisions of position definition and candidate selection. The control by the dean's office was evidenced in these comments by chairmen from a public and a private university:

We have constant problems with replacements here. This year is pretty critical. We have a hard time convincing the college to give us back the money we turn in [from an unused budget line]. In the past the college has kept almost all that money to pay off a deficit. Adding new lines is a different story—that's always a struggle!

It is a very different search environment today from what it was in 1958. There are, for example, all the budget restrictions. We've had to fight hard for positions.

Dean's offices and departments have become conscious of planning— a concept not encountered by Caplow and McGee (although it was certainly anticipated in their work). The dean's requirement of a department plan was mentioned in several instances. Departments themselves used a planning mechanism to make decisions or frame decisionmaking.

Every two years we go off for a weekend retreat and talk about our long-term future, not specifically about people but about research, academics.

We had a three-year program review that was really an intensive process. First we did our own review of the curriculum, then there was an internal review by a three-person committee, people outside of the department, and then there was an external review by three outside chairmen. After all the reports were in, we revised our curriculum. This year every department has had to submit a three-year plan.

This departmental planning, in some cases predating a dean's interest, confirms Cyert's (1982) idea that university planning must be "bottom up"—"That planning works best that has been shaped to a great extent by the faculty in a department" (p. 7). The participatory factor is an important one in the new management strategies.

Management concepts were expressed; indeed, many of the chairmen in this sample viewed themselves as managers in a way that was totally absent from the Caplow and McGee sample. For example, one chairman of a social science department complained that industry did a much better job of recruiting than did universities. He presented his ideas, among them following up a campus visit with a book about the university sent from the provost's office. Others talked about faculty development and motivation, and innovation in their departments. One chairman viewed his management job in this way:

My job as a manager is to enable people to do their work. People need to be made to feel a part of a community of scholars, where they are measured by standards that are mutually agreed upon. Respect for the individual must be maintained in the department. It's important that everyone in the department *participate* in the process.

His concerns about respect for the individual are repeated in these sentiments from two assistant professors:

It is important for a department to recognize junior faculty, and to integrate them into the department. I complain to [the chairman] about that all the time. Named assistant professorships and postdocs are nice methods of recognition.

I feel that tenure chances are pretty good in this department, that the department is very supportive of junior faculty. This is an old, established department and it shows. It is very well run and a good place to be.

A classics chairman had these observations:

We are heavily tenured but productivity after tenure is the responsibility of the chairman. I keep them from becoming stale, they don't teach the same stuff year after year after year. I don't give across-the-board raises. When I have withheld raises, I've had people go out and win major awards. I also give positive reinforcement; some people have blocks about publication, and I try to provide counseling.

And a sociology chairman described one of his management innovations:

For example, we had some problem getting people to teach large classes and that is very important for us because the number of majors is decreasing. So I decided that anyone who taught X number of students a year would get a course off the following year, and it works very well.

There was concern among chairmen at all of the schools about additional layers of bureaucracy interfering with communication:

They told us there were no new positions but we found out accidentally that in fact there were, that some departments were getting them. We have acquired all of this bureaucratic layering. I can't talk to the people I used to talk to, only to the divisional dean.

There is a proliferation of deans. Communication is much more difficult. We have two new associate deans who are just buffers, [to] keep us away from the dean.

Other aspects of institutional management were criticized: for example, a "comparative" salary policy (get an outside offer to get a raise), or this complaint about an ultraconservative budget policy:

The school is generously endowed but it is run by an extremely conservative mentality. One year we underbudgeted badly for heating and they took the money out of everything else rather than just allowing a small deficit.

And a particularly insightful comment on staffing policies:

The academic environment is in serious trouble with respect to one-year appointments. They pay them nothing and they don't incorporate them into the department and there is no development of the organization as a result. The quality of life is poor because of that.

Along with the humdrum day-to-day business, a new management problem has emerged: The chairman is required to deal with sex in academe! Here the comments from both male and female chairmen (wholly unsolicited) ran the gamut from almost scandalous—

She married a colleague who was thrown out of his house by his first wife. The door was actually locked on him. She has a visiting appointment at a local college and is pregnant with twins. This is probably the end of her career, I hope. She should not return to teaching.

She was the mistress of a senior member of another department and collaborated with him professionally. He had pushed her appointment in this department without telling anyone about the personal relationship.

to almost reasonable—

He left voluntarily. He was about to marry one of our graduate students and they got jobs together there. They now have assistant professor positions at a different school.

There was a spouse issue: He was trying to force us to hire his new wife, one of our recent Ph.D.'s. She was at least professional about it here; she had taken him off her committee.

There was one awkwardness in our search. Our in-house candidate that was our own graduate student was very "close," now married, to one of our faculty members, and he was upset that we did not hire her. We need a more formal way of dealing with our own graduate students in the future.

with an interesting (solitary) comment that defies categorization—

She is now married to an emeritus faculty member, the man who was her graduate advisor. She had had a series of romantic interactions with one or more faculty members here. After her first marriage ended in divorce, she married a faculty member, and they were subsequently divorced.

None of the handbooks for department heads cover this topic!

The new academic market bears little resemblance to that of 1958. In his 1983 book, George Keller characterized the introduction of strategic planning into universities as a management revolution in American higher education. His sentiments were summed up neatly in this comment from a chairman of anthropology:

There has been a great change in higher education. You don't run it out of your hip pocket anymore.

3

In Search of the Best

Faculty recruiting is a consuming, gut-wrenching task. It's
very tiring. But we've done an extremely effective job in this
department—our new hires have enhanced our capabilities
enormously, put us on a new track. In spite of the burden, the
department is willing to put the resources into it.

CHAIRMAN OF SOCIOLOGY

Caplow and McGee had remarked that the most striking feature of academic hiring procedures was the time and effort that most departments
devoted to appointments. "The average salary of an assistant professor
is approximately that of a bakery truck driver," they said, "and his
occupancy of a job is likely to be less permanent." But it may take a large
part of the time of several highly skilled people for a long period of time
to hire him. (*Marketplace*, p. 114) That has not changed. The search
process described in this chapter is extremely time-consuming, but it is
viewed by department members as an essential part of their job. The
word "colleague," widely used in academic circles, derives from the
French *legere*, "to choose"—new colleagues must be *chosen* carefully.
This chapter will examine the introduction to the choosing, that is, the
conduct of a faculty search.

Before examining the search itself, however, it is instructive to compare the field and rank of the 1958 searches with those reported in the
1986 study. The searches in the current sample, compared with the
Caplow and McGee data, show two interesting increases: in the natural
sciences and at the full professor level (see Tables 7 and 8). In 1958,
approximately 35 percent of the searches took place in the social sciences
and 28 percent in the natural sciences; in the 1986 sample, the social
sciences proportion had dropped to 31 percent and the natural sciences
increased to 33 percent. The humanities remained about the same.

As to rank, whereas there was little change in the representation of
assistant professors in the study—from a little more than 72 percent to
70 percent—change did occur at the upper ranks. In 1958 associate
professors accounted for almost 18 percent of the search activity and full

Table 7:
Recruiting Departments, by Disciplinary Division and Study

Disciplinary Division	1958 Study		1986 Study	
	No.	%	No.	%
Humanities	24	36.9	33	36.2
Social Studies	23	35.4	28	30.8
Natural Sciences	18	27.7	30	33.0
Total	65	100.0	91	100.0

professors for 10 percent; in 1986 those proportions reversed to 12 percent for associate professors and 18 percent for full professors.

It might be noted here that the difference in the associate professor rank is even greater than indicated because of a split that seems to be occurring in that rank. Four of the seventeen associate professors in the sample were appointed without tenure (in chemistry, economics, philosophy, and physics), a custom being adopted primarily for the pur-

Table 8:
Appointments, by Academic Rank and Study

Academic Rank	1958 Study		1986 Study	
	No.	%	No.	%
Assistant Professor	66	72.5	96	70.1
Associate Professor	16	17.6	17	12.4
Professor	9	9.9	24	17.5
Total	91	100.0	137	100.0

pose of offering a higher salary than could be given an assistant professor, or to provide opportunities for research prior to tenure
consideration. A chairman of economics elaborated in this way:

There is great competition for assistant professors in salary now, and it's probably wise to switch to associate. The starting salary for an assistant is remarkably
close to an associate. Two implications: One, We lose to business schools who
pay $40,000 to $45,000 for an assistant professor; Two, it makes faculty salary
adjustments difficult. I get 4.7 percent to spread around. I try to give the assistant professors more, others go down. I am much more loath to hire assistant
professors.

It was also remarked in conversation that some research universities
purportedly have created an associate professor without tenure rank for
their own faculty members, in order to extend the tenure clock. At some
research universities, it was claimed, associate professors are no longer
tenured—the tenure decision accompanies promotion to full professor.

This turn of events relates to Caplow and McGee's Recommendation
No. 5, wherein they suggested that the period of probation be extended.
That recommendation reflected the market of the times, where demand
had lowered the age for tenure and increased the probability that tenure
would be achieved before the individual's reputation was established.
Therefore, they thought that tenure should not be awarded at "less than
ten years of full-time faculty service, including service on the staff of
another university" (*Marketplace*, p. 244). The realization of this recommendation would appear to be manifested in the current market more
through a weakening than an extension of tenure. In addition to the
untenured associate professors, and although not a formal part of this
study, it is clear from initial data collected from university administrations that non- tenure-track positions are quite popular as an alternative
to long- term commitment of funds for salaries.

So we see that the nature of the search in 1986 may be somewhat
different from that of 1958, especially with the greater emphasis on full
professors and natural scientists. We might hypothesize that the demand for full professors results from a failure to maintain steady flow
through the ranks; the effect of more retirements is beginning to be felt.
As for the ascendance of science, one respondent, a physicist, referred
to what he called the "Toyota revolution"—Japanese industrial competition forcing American attention to science and technology, in much the
same way that the Russian Sputnik acted as a catalyst in an earlier
period.

The balance of this chapter is concerned with the search process: the
beginning—how a position originates and a position description is developed; and the conduct—how news of the opening is communicated,
and what applicants are collected and how they are screened.

ORIGINATION OF THE POSITION

Caplow and McGee referred to an assumption about budget lines, or "slots," and a vacancy-and-replacement attitude that had a faculty departure triggering a faculty replacement at the same rank within the same department, almost automatically. Their Recommendation No. 11 called for a faculty vacancy to be based on need rather than right of succession. The situation they described no longer exists, and in fact probably has not existed for years. In this study, the opening being filled was frequently not a direct replacement (except in budget terms) for a departed faculty member; often it was a composite or a choice made to strengthen the department, and sometimes it was a newly defined position designed to meet new needs within the department.

In any case, the academic department was not given a replacement position automatically but was required to request authorization to recruit from the dean (usually, sometimes other academic administrators were involved), and that authorization could be negotiated in some detail: rank, field, term of appointment, tenure status, salary range. Detailed negotiation was not a hard and fast rule, and there were a number of instances in the sample where the department began recruiting very broadly, and some where lack of initial success resulted in changing the specifications. In several senior appointments, the person was located before the authorization was requested, that is, it was learned that a senior person might be available and authorization to recruit the specific individual was sought. Infrequently, the opening was initiated by a dean or provost—for example, an incoming senior professor was accommodated by giving the department several junior positions to fill, or a need in an interdisciplinary program was assigned to a particular department—but the recruiting process was the department's responsibility.

Opening gambits were described by this chairman:

The chairman writes letters to the dean and doesn't really expect to get a position, but if you persist long enough, you usually get it. The best justification is on teaching load.

Departmental views of the authorization process could vary, however, as witness these two comments from the same university:

If there is no change in the total number, we just tell the dean [that we are going to recruit]—we assume a permanent roster.

We react to signals from the dean's office. The dean lets us know what we can do, and then we try to work around to what we need.

DESCRIPTION OF THE POSITION

Prior to a request for authorization it was necessary for the department to decide what it wanted. Methods for accomplishing this varied slightly across institutions and across disciplinary divisions, but especially across individual departments, with different effects even in similar departments. For example, in two small humanities departments in different universities, the respective chairmen commented:

The department had several meetings to decide whether we wanted someone in the same field. The department was able to reach consensus without *loud* disagreement.

The department had a retreat at a conference center—one and a half days—we were really in solitary confinement. There we developed a five-year plan.

And in two larger social science departments:

I [the chairman] poll the faculty and compile the statistical summary of the distribution and I look at that along with teaching needs. Then I work with the executive committee consisting of two persons of each rank plus two graduate students and make the decision.

A departmental meeting was called to set priorities—we discuss and fight!

A number of chairmen described quite deliberate processes, as in these comments from the social sciences:

It starts with the subdiscipline. Our department is divided into physical anthropology, archaeology, social anthropology, and cultural anthropology. The particular group meets and decides what it wants and then the department as a whole discusses it. Those outside the group are looking for some kind of validation. It tends to be discussed at great length. Sometimes we set up a presearch committee just to see what's out there in the field.

There are seven or eight areas in the department—clinical, social, developmental, experimental, etc. Positions tend to be viewed by areas as their own. We made a conscious decision about twelve or so years ago to build the developmental area and that reflects some planning. This keeps internecine warfare down to a dull roar.

Most departments that are large enough have organized themselves in ways to facilitate decisionmaking:

We have an executive committee elected by the whole department nominated within certain groups, and that committee meets with the chairman and then they vote. The committee is advisory to the chairman. The chairman can go against their wishes but he better have a good reason or he loses his credibility.

We have a table of organization here, essentially, determined by the nature of the discipline—like a baseball team has to have nine people on the field.

Now and then the team approach did not work:

It was a complex search conducted in two separate fields. The department couldn't agree on what was needed.

The department doesn't arrive at a consensus until it starts looking!

Even in those institutions where departmental "executive committees" were prescribed, the results were not uniform:

There is input to the executive committee through the five division coordinators. The executive committee in this department consists of the full professors and they make the decision on what we are going to do.

Our executive committee consists of five professors, three associate professors, and two assistant professors, who are elected by the faculty. One of their regular orders of business in the late spring or early fall is to decide what kinds of vacancies we are going to have.

Nevertheless, a clear pattern emerged as to the level in the academic department where the decision about the nature of the opening was made. The pattern can be seen in the analysis of decision levels in the ninety-one recruiting departments, as shown in Table 9, as among full faculty, committee, or chairman. Although there was a slight proportional bent toward committee decision in public universities and in larger departments, about 60 percent of the departments sampled enjoyed full faculty participation in the decision and the overall effect was one of democracy in action.

COMMUNICATION

Caplow and McGee complained about "information screens" that prevented departments from having knowledge of prospective applicants and prospective applicants from having knowledge about openings, and recommended (No. 8) that this condition be rectified. They described "nepotistic themes" as a heavy contributor to this state of affairs: e.g., help from the home institution, knowing or being known by someone influential in the hiring, having some previous connection with the institution. More than half the assistant professors and more than 60 percent of the associate and full professors in their sample had made no overt efforts to locate their jobs but were individually pursued by the hiring department.

A change has occurred, however, at the initiation of the search. Faculty recruitment in the 1980s, with few exceptions, begins with advertis-

Table 9:
Decision Level of Faculty Position Definition

| | Number of Departments | | | | |
| | Decision Level | | | | |
Unit of Comparison	Full Faculty	Committee	Chairman	Special	Total
Institution:					
Public	27	14	6	6	53
Private	27	4	2	5	38
Total	54	18	8	11	91
Disciplinary Division:					
Humanities	20	7	1	4	32
Social Sciences	17	4	4	4	29
Natural Sciences	17	7	3	3	30
Total	54	18	8	11	91
Department Size:					
Small	24	1	-	5	30
Medium	26	9	5	3	43
Large	4	8	3	3	18
Total	54	18	8	11	91

ing; the search is public knowledge and there is no evidence that the apparent openness of the process is deceptive: "The process is more open because of the wider advertising," said one chairman. Every department surveyed (with the exception of special situations, to be discussed later) began its search by preparing and placing an advertisement in a professional journal customarily read by job-seekers in the discipline. Some went so far as to advertise additionally in more general publications such as the *Chronicle of Higher Education*. One suspects that Brown's (1967) and others' assertions that knowledge of the academic job market is constrained by lack of communication are no longer valid; if anything, knowledge of the opening is overcommunicated.

Differing opinions about results from ads in journals were expressed by chairmen. The views are typified by these two comments from the natural sciences at the same university, both relating to searches at the assistant professor level, and both from departments ranked in the top ten:

At the junior level, sometimes there are surprises from the ads, people that we wouldn't turn up otherwise.

No one ever shows up from the ads that we didn't already know about; the ads satisfy the legal requirements.

The value of open advertising is confirmed by the fact that of the seventy-four assistant professors interviewed for this study, forty had obtained their positions by responding to advertisements in professional journals*. One assistant professor in computer science remarked that when he started looking around, "There were five hundred ads and you skimmed through to see what you would like to apply for."

The experience of assistant professors, however, did not hold across ranks. Among associate professors, only four out of fourteen responded to advertisements; at full professor rank, only four out of twenty indicated that they had learned about the job through an advertisement.

Additional open advertising took place through notices of openings sent to other departments at institutions granting the Ph.D. in that particular discipline. According to new-appointee respondents, these notices were often posted on bulletin boards by the recipients.

Although the process could be characterized as universalistic up to this point, it then became particularistic. The chairman of a social sciences department ranked number one said:

---

*The other thirty-four had heard about the position, before seeing an ad, from personal contacts such as a major advisor or a friend on the searching faculty. It is not certain that this prior knowledge had any effect on their success, however, nor was there any pattern as to department ranking of Ph.D. or job.

I think the most effective recruitment method is my phoning, beating the bushes, going to meetings. This year I am going to two meetings although we will not be recruiting until next year.

From a physics department in the top fifteen came this admission:

We advertised just in case, but our recruitment source was really "old boy." Everybody is known to each other in high energy physics. They come from four or five sources. (There was a woman finalist.)

In almost all cases, the department members made telephone calls to persons known at other institutions in order to call the opening to their attention and try to ensure that their best people applied. (This method has the socially acceptable label of "networking," as opposed to the socially unacceptable "old-boy network." Presumably the web now includes old girls.) As noted earlier, about 46 percent of the assistant professors interviewed reported hearing about the job through some kind of personal contact: a colleague, a graduate advisor, a faculty member in the searching department, or by being "in place" in the relevant department as a visiting faculty member or in a postdoctoral fellowship. Virtually all of the persons appointed at the senior level mentioned such contacts.

Neither inbreeding (hiring one's own Ph.D.'s) nor outbreeding or "silver-cording" (hiring one's own Ph.D.'s after they have served an initial apprenticeship or established a career elsewhere), both characteristics noted by Caplow and McGee and later by Brown (1967), loomed large in the current investigation. Only three assistant professors, two associate professors, and two professors had earned their doctorates at the employing institution. Further removed, five assistant professors and one professor had been undergraduates; two assistant professors had siblings who had been undergraduates there.

The once prevalent method of placement by a mentor at the "right place" also seems to have vanished. One chairman related an anecdote contrasting past and present procedures:

There's the old story told in Slavic languages about the senior scholar in the field. If you wanted to fill a job you got on the phone to him and asked him for someone and he would ruminate and then say, "I gif you Joe Smith."

Another expressed relief at no longer being

at the mercy of a senior man here who has a friend somewhere with a graduate student he wants to place.

And another added an element of objectivity to the networking:

We call people at the top twenty or so places—the placement person plus one or two others to keep them honest.

The minority opinion was that things were better in the old days via the old ways. A chairman in the humanities talked nostalgically about his practice twenty years before:

It was much easier and more certain fifteen to twenty years ago. I could take a trip, drop in here and there, come back, report, the staff would decide, and then we went to the dean and hired somebody.

A social sciences chairman believed that the old-boy network of years past had produced better candidates. And chairmen in the natural sciences and social sciences remarked on the current mix of procedures:

We end up with the same candidates. It [current search procedure] broadens the pool, but when we get down to the wire it's the same system. There is no depth in the pool.

We recruit from the top twenty departments. If we didn't advertise at all, we would get the same people.

Another chairman described the present procedure as "rounding up all the suspects," and in this study the suspects were rounded up through advertising that could be quite detailed or quite vague, depending upon several factors, or as one chairman put it: "Well, it depends on which year it is, the phase of the moon and all that!" As a general rule, larger departments tended to advertise less well defined openings; smaller departments with precise teaching or research needs and fewer people to cover them were more specific in their job descriptions. A chairman of one of the latter type said, "Even the course load was specified in the ad!" Advertisements for senior positions were also less well defined.

Always, there was a concern for quality. This concern was often a unifying factor in the search:

We want quality, in broadly defined areas. The quality element is overwhelmingly important in this department. You decide you need a quarterback, and then a lot of people think the defensive end is the better person. The quality standard overrides that.

In many instances, there was an acknowledgment that if a superb person showed up, the department might display a certain amount of flexibility in retailoring the job needs:

We often look for anybody anywhere at the junior level. The department is attracted by intelligence.

The committee set some general priorities about fields but we also just have to go after the opportunities that come along to get the people who are top rate. We don't go out hiring for a field and compromise quality.

Generally we know what our needs are, but we are open to exceptional people.

And in spite of the organized orderliness of the process, the search for quality can provide a serendipitous element even, in this case, in a top-ranked biology department:

We didn't know about [the successful candidate]. Someone heard about her. All of our methodical searching didn't turn her up. Her Ph.D. advisor was one of our graduate students, but he was not on our nominator list.

APPLICANT POOLS

Needless to say, broad communication of information about the opening coupled with market changes generate large applicant pools, especially at the junior level. In Caplow and McGee's 1958 sample the majority of the positions filled had ten or fewer candidates. In the current market, the situation is far different. For example, the sociology search for three assistant professors described by Smelser and Content (1980) netted 285 candidates. Questions about applicant pools for assistant professor openings at these six universities elicited the information that two-thirds of the departments typically attracted more than fifty applications for an assistant professor opening, and over a third attracted more than a hundred applications (see Table 10).

Academic departments have devised efficient ways of dealing with the large applicant flow. Larger departments might have standing recruitment committees, frequently one for senior and one for junior appointments. In others, chairmen appointed ad hoc search committees whose composition varied. Some chairmen preferred a search committee consisting of specialists in the field; some put an outsider from another field on the committee "to keep them honest." In a few large departments with well-defined subspecialties, the group within which the position would be located chose its own committee. One chairman talked about his "anarchic" department: "I don't make any assignments, people are interested and they step forward and do the work." Occasionally the search committee extended outside of the department in order to draw upon expertise located elsewhere in the university or to accommodate an interdisciplinary focus.

The expansion of the junior applicant pool is no doubt affected by three factors working in combination: the dissemination of knowledge of the opening, the increase in Ph.D. production since the late 1950s, and the decrease in total number of academic openings since 1970. There is not, however, a direct relationship between the increase in the num-

Table 10:
Typical Number of Applications for Assistant Professor Position, by
Disciplinary Division

Disciplinary Division	Number of Departments Number of Applications				
	Fewer Than 50	50-100	100-200	More Than 200	Total
Humanities	12	5	6	3	26
Social Sciences	7	9	8	2	26
Natural Sciences	5	4	8	4	21
Total	24	18	22	9	73

ber of Ph.D.'s produced and the number of applicants for academic jobs. The National Research Council (1983) reported that 46.7 percent of the total of 23,833 Ph.D.'s produced in 1969 planned to seek academic employment, but only 31.9 percent of the 28,716 produced in 1983 planned to do so. Thus, the actual numbers dropped from 11,130 in 1969 to 9,160 in 1983. Decreases are reflected in all fields. For example, there was a drop in real numbers from 946 to 526 in the biological and health sciences, and from 1,968 to 1,606 in the social sciences. In addition, the number of Ph.D.'s produced has decreased in some fields and has been accompanied by a decrease in the proportion going into academe. In the humanities, for example, the total number dropped from 3,585 to 3,292, and the proportion seeking academic employment dropped from 73.8 percent to 45.9 percent. Similar declines occurred in physics and astronomy, chemistry, and mathematics. Consequently, it is likely that the larger applicant pools are more a function of the broader advertising of jobs than of more Ph.D.'s. Confirming this point, Bowen and Schuster (1986) found little unemployment of Ph.D.'s, and Youn (1981) observed that supply has less influence on the academic labor market than demand. This can be an important consideration as demand increases in the 1990s.

As might be expected, applicant pools at the associate and full professor levels rarely attracted a large applicant (or nominee) pool. As one respondent noted, "The big question in a senior search is, who can we get?" This account by a professor of his recruitment is revealing:

It was really interesting how I got this job. My friend Smith is an outstanding scientist, and the fact that he was interested in the job and clearly had an

outstanding offer from here made me think about this school for the first time. Then I heard that he had decided to stay where he was and not come here. I was on leave at the time, and when I heard that Smith wasn't going to take the job, my wife and I drove up here and looked around the campus. After that we had the possibility of moving on the brain. I had seen their advertisement by then, but my father had been an administrator and taught me that for a senior position, one never approaches directly. So I called a friend at another school and asked about this job, said I thought I would be interested; I had heard that Smith wasn't going to accept the offer and when he turned it down I thought I would take a crack at it. My intermediary said, are you sure? But I said that I had talked to Smith only yesterday and he said that he had turned the job down. I then asked my friend if he would approach them for me, sent him my c.v., and he sent it on. Then Smith told me that he took the job. He had wanted to wait for his kids to get older but when he heard that I was interested in the job, he realized that it might not be on the market for the couple of years that he had wanted them to wait for him, and so he accepted. Then they called and said that Smith accepted, but they hoped that this was the first of several appointments. And they ended up hiring both of us.

INITIAL SCREENING

Search and screen committees, no matter how constituted, set about their business of sorting out the candidates in a remarkably similar manner, differentiated only by the level of the search. Their "regular, orderly procedures" have fulfilled Caplow and McGee's ninth recommendation, as noted in this quote from a chairman of geography at a state university:

The search process is much more thorough and much more formalized. The process itself should yield the best candidate. Great care is given to analysis of records; all materials are read. It used to be run in a much more informal manner.

First, the materials describing the candidates were assembled: curricula vitae, including lists of publications and statements of research plans, and letters of recommendation or references (the latter because some departments liked to request the letters themselves). The first cut was often made by the committee on the basis of the candidate's specialization or research interests or, in the case of a junior appointment, the improbability of completion of the doctorate by the specified appointment date. (Two departments screened *first* on thesis materials.) It was noted by most respondents that the letters of recommendation were extremely important as a screening device. Lewis (1975) has pointed out at length the shortcomings of letters of recommendation, commenting that such letters are a "ritualistic exercise used only to confirm what the reader wants to confirm," and that the writers tend to say what they think the department wants them to say about the candidate (p. 50).

Nevertheless, in this academic world of uncertainty about professional potential, letters of recommendation remained paramount in the search criteria. As in the earlier period studied by Caplow and McGee, the identity of the author is important:

Letters count for a lot, good letters by writers with some reputation. The field is small enough that letters are not taken lightly. We know everybody who's writing.

They [the search committee] read the letters of recommendation for the first screening. Extra weight is given for letters from truly distinguished people.

Letters are valued highly but selectively—it depends on who is writing it.

But note occasional reservations:

Letters are very important. . . . But sometimes you get real duds and you wonder how many you missed because of the importance you placed on letters.

Letters are significant *even though they are inflated* and it is who writes them that is important.

And there were attempts to validate the information contained in the letters:

We asked for more than three references because we don't get replies from everybody and want at least three. There was a fair amount of phoning. If you trust the person that you phone, that's very often very useful.

We ask for letters and we follow up the letters with phone calls.

There was some disparity in the data as to the importance of letters of recommendation in a senior search; both of the following comments came from chemistry departments not ranked in the top ten:

We depend fairly strongly on outside letters. We will solicit opinions from people we know in the field, ask for comparison with leaders in the field. I [the chairman] write these letters myself.

The letters are important for the deans and the provost! We don't pay much attention to letters, we think we know the best people—Nobel Laureates, members of the National Academy, etc.

At the junior level, screening continued by obtaining (if not already in hand) and *reading* samples of the candidate's writing. Reading the work was apparently so infrequent in Caplow and McGee's sample that one of their recommendations (No. 8) called for improving existing procedures by seeing that the "professional publications of the candidate, including

especially his doctoral dissertation, be *read*." (*Marketplace*, p. 249) To-day's evaluators, with few exceptions, read the candidate's work.

The screening committee farms out to the appropriate members of the faculty various papers. The search committee reads the c.v. and the letters and then the papers of about twenty to thirty people. The whole faculty reads papers of the visitors.

The search committee screened down to ten or twelve and asked for disserta-tions which the committee read. Then we screened to three and everyone read those dissertations.

We are terrible about hiring people. We pick them over, we *read* their thesis. If it's not publishable, we are not interested.

For a senior person we read the work very, very carefully.

In the humanities, social sciences, and selected natural sciences, the writing sample was almost always the doctoral thesis or chapters from the doctoral thesis, which was judged on the basis of topic—"the disser-tation subject is the most important thing"—as well as research and writing ability. In those natural sciences where postdoctoral fellowships are common or required, writing beyond the dissertation was expected:

We prefer diversity in the research. We like people to have done a Ph.D. in one thing and a postdoc in another and have been successful in both.

At the end of the screening, the search committee presented to the department either a "short list" to be reduced further by the full faculty, or a list of prospects for campus visits. An intermediate step in some departments was the interviewing of candidates at the national meeting of a professional association, although this was not consistent across a discipline and seemed to be influenced by the chairman's attitude to-ward interviewing at national meetings. As one humanities chairman indicated:

Recruitment is tough, a time-consuming job. Our procedures are very elaborate in order to insure fairness. This is really the most important thing one does, though, maintaining the quality of the department. Conventions matter less—there is no slave market anymore.

At the senior level, although letters of recommendation may remain an important prerequisite to appointment, the members of the depart-ment are usually familiar with the candidate's work and are often more intent on convincing him or her to take the job than in deliberating over qualifications. "The most important credential is, would he have any

interest in coming here?" Rather extraordinary attempts at identification may be made:

We considered full professors in the field. . . . We got a little ghoulish—for example, looking at who just got divorced and might want to move.

The senior search process is more ascriptive at the outset, as illustrated by this comment from a chemistry department:

We did a lot of phoning around and talked to the three senior people in this country plus the senior person in England and the senior person in Germany. We surveyed names from the programs of two international meetings.

Throughout the search process, at any level, the full departmental faculty was welcomed and encouraged to read the files, express opinions to members of the search committee, and argue for inclusion or exclusion of candidates. Formal procedures were used by some departments:

There are two people in charge of recruiting. We start out with about 150 names that we have screened down from the total applicants [for more than one junior position]. There are regular workshops by field with two or three people responsible for each field. Review sheets are filled out by the faculty.

In other departments, proceedings were less formal:

The search committee has the initial job of shaking the bushes, calling, writing, etcetera to make sure that all the good people apply. They then whittle the list down but the faculty are given a "white ball" and can put anyone back on the short list.

Again, we find a highly participatory decision making process. As one experienced chairman commented:

I've been chairman here for a long time, before that chairman of another department, before that chairman at another university. If there is a lesson to be learned, it is that you can never please everybody all the time, but if there is one place where you have to be democratic, it's in selecting new faculty.

WHAT ROLE AFFIRMATIVE ACTION?

Although bias was a concern of Caplow and McGee, their book was published almost a decade before passage of the Civil Rights Act of 1964, and before President Johnson signed Executive Order 11246 in 1965. The "affirmative action" required by the Executive Order, although ambiguous for higher education until employment law was specifically extended to cover professionals in 1972, created new rules and regulations

governing the search process. Consequently, the interview schedule for the study was modified to include the question, "What effect do institutional affirmative action requirements have on your recruiting?"

Responses indicated that the impact point of affirmative action on the search process appears to have passed, that is, the current effect of affirmative action on the recruitment process is minimal. The words "institutionalized" and "internalized" were used again and again to describe affirmative action; less positive terms were "legalistic" and "tedious":

Affirmative action has become institutionalized. Perhaps ten years ago it made a difference.

There are tedious requirements. There are endless explanations required for candidates that are not worth it. It's hard to say whether affirmative action makes a difference. Perhaps initially it made us more aware of the problem.

In the ninety-one recruiting departments sampled, a large majority did not consider their searches to be affected by institutional affirmative action requirements (see Table 11).

The factor apparently most closely associated with the success of affirmative action is the commitment of the individual department to the concept. Thus, although it is a relatively new addition to the search procedure, affirmative action relies upon the traditional responsibility of the department for the recruitment process:

There are requirements on the books, and it's really a matter of making it known that we are an equal opportunity employer. It is a matter of intent versus legal-

Table 11:
Effect of Affirmative Action Requirements on Recruiting, by Department

	Departments	
Effect	No.	%
Department exceeds requirements	14	15.4
Not much effect	43	47.3
No effect at all	21	23.1
Negative effect	10	11.0
Other (specific effect)	3	3.2
Total	91	100.0

ism and what's crucial is intent. You do something legalistic so you can put
something down, and then you make the real attempt otherwise.

Departmental responsibility is further underscored by the fact that the
chairmen who were most positive about the philosophy of affirmative
action divorced themselves from the actual administration of affirmative
action on their campus.

We would not have chosen her if we did not feel she was best, but when I
became chairman there were no women in the department. We have four right
now (out of twenty). The requirements on this campus are nothing, all paperwork. They set goals but we could always say that other people were more
qualified. It is necessary to have the right attitude in the key people, not present
it as a bureaucratic chore.

Well, I think the department is itself quite committed to making a genuine
affirmative action effort. It is department policy that the committee present the
top woman and the top black regardless of where they rank. The department
has a fair number of social activists—we were very active in the Vietnam War
and in efforts to expand the size of the black student body. At present we have
three female colleagues, all quite recent but all tenured now. The dean doesn't
care about the issue.

We have been trying to follow affirmative action guidelines which the department reformulated for itself last year. There has been some feeling by members
of the department that we weren't doing as much as we should have done. This
year there is much more awareness in the junior recruiting committee that we
need to take a serious look for minority candidates and women. This year we
had two women and one minority candidate in our final group. That's on our
own initiative.

In similar but more emphatic vein, we encounter these comments:

The affirmative action requirements in general are a big albatross around our
neck, probably the worst thing about hiring here, creates a very cumbersome
process. It has mostly negative effects. We need people as chairmen who are
genuinely interested; that is the only way to progress affirmative action.

Of the nineteen faculty members in this department, three are women, two are
blacks, and two are Chicanos. We will almost certainly add one to two women
this year. The affirmative action requirements on this campus are not effective.
The general stress on affirmative action is helpful, the financial support is helpful. The campus program for minority fellowships for postdocs is helpful; we
appointed somebody out of that program. The special slot for affirmative action
is helpful. Bureaucratic details are *not* helpful. They slow things down and there
are all sorts of petty annoyances. The reporting requirements are cumbersome.
It is just a pain in the neck. The legalistic interpretations really create a backlash.
I believe that general pressure for affirmative action is good, but when the
lawyers get into the picture, they screw it up.

A few chairmen considered the formal affirmative action requirements on their campuses superficial, as indicated in this response: "We called the 'positive action office' or whatever it's called to do the legal thing."

Two women and one black male in the sample thought that their appointments were related to affirmative action. One of the women said:

There is still a lingering feeling in this department about preferring a male. I was really their second choice, but the administration would not pass on the male they wanted.

Her opinion was not entirely confirmed by her chairman, who said that some members of the department felt that she got the job because she was a woman, but it was his opinion that her publications were more impressive. It seemed that this was a departmental conflict about the professional qualifications of the candidate, with affirmative action overtones, that was pushed up to the dean level for resolution.

The philosophical arguments of the early 1970s (e.g., Hook 1974, Lester 1974) have waned; there was little argument presented by the chairmen against affirmative action. Their complaints focused on the administration of the affirmative action program within the institution. Two chairmen did claim affirmative action to be irrelevant, however—they searched for the best regardless of skin color or anatomical structure, they said. One other chairman stated his views unequivocally: "I am from Germany and I find this male-female stuff *nonsense.*"

And although there was some question as to whether the current degree of acceptance of women and minorities in academe would have occurred without affirmative action, there was also a suggestion from some chairmen that it may have had more effect, at least for women, at the training rather than the hiring level. Affirmative action requirements are viewed primarily as preliminary to the selection process—the applicant pool is broadened. While this has worked to the advantage of women as the number of Ph.D.'s awarded to women has increased, it has had disappointing results for those minorities (blacks and Hispanics) who are underrepresented in graduate schools. Compare these statements:

In our field women have become increasingly evident. We don't have to pay special attention to them. We have two tenured women in this department. We have made offers to two women in this year's searches.

We would go after a black vigorously if we could find one to go after.

In view of the fact that the results have been limited for blacks, and the forecast for the group is not optimistic, one wonders if societal changes (e.g., a shift to a service-based economy and subsequent aspirations and

preparation of women for more responsible jobs) should be given the most credit for the change that has occurred. Broadening an applicant pool according to affirmative action dicta gains nothing where applicants are scarce. Indeed, there was considerable lament over the scarce supply of black Ph.D.'s, and one black professor acknowledged:

The job market for a half dozen black people is fantastic. There are unlimited opportunities for good blacks if they go to the right schools.

In spite of the universal complaint about the paperwork connected with the administration of the affirmative action program, one chairman conjectured: "The paperwork reminds us of the intent and perhaps motivates us to be more attentive." And perhaps because of the paperwork required, affirmative action seemed firmly fixed in many minds in its relationship to the advertising of positions, which almost everyone agreed was desirable. Dissenting opinions were heard from a few chairmen, including this one in mathematics:

I believe that advertising has desirable societal ends, but it's a waste of money. The kind of people we want to hire are in some instances too shy, in a way, to apply. We generate lists of names by brainstorming.

Some chairmen, too, thought that routine advertising, at least of junior positions, began some years before affirmative action, as higher education expanded explosively in the 1960s and the "old boy network" was strained beyond its capacity:

The job listing in our professional journal has evolved to a far more comprehensive vehicle; positions are far more widely advertised. I think this is due to the growth of the field, just the numbers. To my recollection it has not been any different for the sixteen years that I've been here.

I think that advertising predated affirmative action. We are not doing anything different. There has been advertising with the professional associations ever since the job listing was started. I believe that market changes were the impetus for advertising.

Further, the difficulty of comparing then and now was pointed out by a senior professor:

Back in the 50's it looked like an old boy network but it really wasn't. There were just fewer of us. The American Astronomical Society had 800 members when I was treasurer; now there are 3600. When I became treasurer, I knew every graduate student in the country personally. It was a totally different world back then.

And some remarked on the influence of professional associations:

The Linguistic Society recommends advertising, and they would refuse to carry the ad of any university not an affirmative action employer.

The APA has a blacklist of schools that are guilty of discriminatory practices, not advertising positions, etc.

But generally, this remark was typical:

I suppose the important thing is advertising. We are much more confident that we seem to be objective. We feel more comfortable about it. There is an awareness without really thinking about it. We sometimes say there aren't enough women in this pool of applicants and we have gone back and checked ourselves. In the early seventies we hired our first woman and one of our department members said, "Over my dead body." Then there was a period of readjustment. We redefined ourselves and we all benefited from that. I think we are at the point now where our self-identification is very well generalized and the gender and racial diversity in the department is taken for granted and isn't even thought about.

There were clear differences in the responses to questions about affirmative action according to the style of affirmative action administration on the campus. At one public university and one private university, where the requirements were viewed as stringent, intrusive, and largely unnecessary, there seemed to be some resentment shown toward affirmative action objectives. At the other four schools, where the internal procedures were significantly more low-keyed, there was more of an accepted awareness of the social necessity of affirmative action and less irritation with procedure.

Many departments took pride in their affirmative action results, as evidenced by this quote from a chairman of English:

We are very proud of the fact that we have eight or nine good women who are publishing good things. I think we are exceptional among the top schools in that respect.

Perhaps the most telling observation, though, was made by one chairman who said:

I read the publications of the organizations of women faculty on this campus and feel that they are preoccupied with the same issues of ten years ago that are no longer pressing issues. It is not difficult for women any more. But the question is what it's going to mean in twenty years to be a university professor. [This university] has a two-tiered structure, stars and others, and the others hire as cheaply as possible and keep as cheaply as possible.

4

New Patterns of Choice

We know instantly when we are up against a really good mind. The quality of mind is not difficult to sort out. I quote Housman: "I can no more define poetry than a terrier can a rat, but I fancy we both know it when we see it."

FORMER CHAIRMAN OF CLASSICS

In the last chapter we looked at the way in which a faculty position is defined by the recruiting department and the procedures used in searching for candidates. This chapter carries the process of choosing to completion, in the selection and appointment of the new faculty member. We find both parties to the choice taking great care.

As was noted about the search, there is some variation in the process as it relates to rank, that is, different procedures apply to junior and senior appointments. For example, we saw that applicant pools were quite large and that advertising was an effective recruiting method for junior positions. Applicant pools were much smaller for senior positions, and senior faculty members were not effectively recruited through public advertising. As will be seen in the following discussion, the close of the recruitment process differs by rank as well. As noted earlier in Table 8, the great majority of hiring activity—almost three-fourths of the total—occurred at the assistant professor rank.

SELECTION OF ASSISTANT PROFESSORS

Looking at the final stage of the recruitment process of an assistant professor, we find at the outset a difference from 1958. Less than half of the assistant professors in Caplow and McGee's sample were interviewed prior to being hired. In the current study, there was general agreement that the interview was the pinnacle of the upward climb for the junior faculty candidate—the place where the candidate could perform brilliantly or self-destruct. There was little variation across departments, but the following were exceptions: Four of the departments in the sample conducted interviews only at professional meetings and did

not invite candidates to visit the campus; one chairman explained in this way:

> The interviews were conducted by all of us [who attended the meeting] interviewing in a group. There is only a campus visit if there is some controversy. We present the case to the department and the department votes.

In three other cases, the campus visit was relatively undemanding, as exemplified in these comments:

> We have become disenchanted with lectures and we try to put the candidates in different environments, that is, small groups by field, with graduate students, etcetera, and then everyone who has met the candidate comments.

> We don't ask junior candidates to make a presentation. We tried that in the past, but they are too nervous and they generally just present something from their dissertation that we can read anyway, and it just doesn't work. We want to make sure they know what they are getting into before they come here, and much of our effort during the visit is spent in explaining to them what we do and what we expect of them and trying to determine whether this fits in with their career plans.

But for the large majority of the new appointees, the job search culminated in an experience described by one chairman as "grueling" and by an assistant professor as "intensive." The routine was fairly standard across the departments surveyed, and activity fell roughly into three categories: group professional, individual professional, and semi-social. The group professional activity, viewed by many as the most important, was the presentation—or in some cases two presentations, one informal to faculty members and graduate students with research interests similar to those of the candidate, and the more formal presentation to a larger group that might include members of other departments. The job talk, as it often is called, was seen as an indication of classroom performance as well as the candidate's ability to communicate research results. In a psychology department at a private university:

> We give *much weight* to the presentation. We are very concerned with teaching at the undergraduate level.

In a history department at another private university:

> The critical thing is the departmental seminar which consists of a thirty- to forty-minute talk including twenty to thirty minutes on current research, ten minutes on future research, ten minutes on what they want to teach. Then there is a rigorous question and answer period. We have two faculty members who ask the incisive questions and we listen very carefully to how they handle those questions.

In a classics department at a public university:

There was a talk at noon in the lounge to which students came. We are interested in whether they can lecture and how they would interact with the University community, especially students.

In a zoology department at another public university:

The informal seminar with colleagues can be blue skying but the formal one where students are present had better not be.

The individual professional meetings could be arranged in different ways: "office hours" held by the candidate, a prearranged appointment schedule developed from faculty and graduate student signup sheets, less formal meetings made possible by size in smaller departments. In four universities in the sample, appointments were arranged with deans or associate deans, who "talked with the candidates about teaching"; in two private universities in the sample, administrators met only with candidates for tenured appointments. (Several assistant professor interviewees mentioned the meeting with the dean as a plus for the university.) It would be an exaggeration to classify the individual meetings within the department as job interviews. It was generally conceded by chairmen, and corroborated by assistant professors, that the "interview" more often consisted of the faculty member talking about his own research than querying the candidate. There was also a good deal of attention paid to acclimatizing the candidate: "We tell them what life is like here."

The semi-social category covered approximately everything else that occurred during the candidate's visit. The chairman might take him out for a beer (no hers were accorded this treatment); the graduate students might take the candidate out for pizza; the search committee or some other combination of departmental people would buy him or her lunch, and dinner, and breakfast. There were receptions including spouses (one chairman said of the successful candidate, "my wife liked her") and one particularly sensitive chairman arranged dinner for the candidates with the assistant professors in the department. The candidates were shown the town, and some got to meet real estate agents. But the semi-social had to be considered very semi; as one candid chairman remarked, "We entertain them socially and we try to grill them as we do that."

In fact, the visit is very much a test of whether the candidate will fit in as a colleague. The visit permits firsthand examination of the qualities that the department is seeking:

Where is the graduate work done; who is writing for the candidate? Are they doing interesting, exciting work? We give high priority to two other things: One,

teaching. We are a state university and teaching is important to us. Two, this is a collegial department and we want someone who will fit in, not be a "bad apple." We can't find out about these two things until the very end of the process.

Collegiality is quite important. The autonomy of a faculty position and the lack of socializing devices within the department make it important for the candidate to display at least some of the characteristics that will lead the members of the department to identify him or her with their ideas and beliefs. The following comments from three different schools and three different disciplines in three different parts of the country are revealing:

Then there is the very important personal time spent with the candidate—for example, driving to and from the airport.

He [the successful candidate] stayed at my house on his visit to campus. You have to get to know them, you are choosing a colleague.

It [the interview process] is a quasi-mating dance.

Yet, the basis of choice—that clincher that gets the job—was rarely described in personal terms by the chairpersons interviewed. Quality of research, the dissertation, and especially the presentation—style, competence, substance—were important factors. Humanists were looking for breadth, the unusual expertise, originality, and poise and warmth in communication:

She has an unusual background; she is an Andeanist as well as Spanish. We hadn't had anybody who had that sort of interest. Finally, she has a pleasant personality, an engaging style, good presentation.

Social scientists were placing a premium on quantitative methodology, but also were looking for creativity, style, and depth:

He came from a school that is highly regarded in macroeconomics, trained by one of the three top people. They turn out a type of macroeconomist that is much admired. The only problem is that they could be clones of their teachers and we worry about that. Smith showed a refreshing independence. We also want someone who can get off their specialty and talk good sensible economics, someone with depth and adaptability, and he displayed that.

Natural scientists were attracted by independence as well:

We were very much attracted by his area of research. We needed someone in the central nervous system. We also liked his evolutionary approach. His postdoc worried us a little, but we became convinced through many discussions with him and his mentor that he was independent.

Across disciplines there was recognition of personal dynamism ("We don't want a recluse in this department"), *spirit*, excitement about their work—as one chairman called it, "fire in the eyes."

It is refreshing to note, in spite of the governing selection criterion of research orientation, the emphasis on teaching in these major research universities: commitment to teaching, teaching experience, and a presentation that displays a potential for teaching were mentioned frequently. These are quotes from a private and two public universities:

We ask for evidence of teaching performance, teaching evaluations. We take teaching very seriously. One can't get a job in this department on the basis of research alone.

I think probably the main issue was the expectation we had of teaching. She had been a teaching assistant and also had taught French. She promised to be a very competent teacher. She had considerable breadth. The runner-up had good scholarly quality but we had doubts about his teaching.

We don't hire anyone who is not a good teacher no matter how brilliant he is.

This is not to suggest that research is not the principal emphasis in hiring, as was made clear in this statement—

We don't want a poor teacher, but the top 50 percent is okay, whereas we want the top 1 percent in research.

and elaborated upon in these:

In talking about research and teaching you have to understand that students are involved in 99 percent of the research.

Teaching experience is important; in this field there is a heavy teaching load. But a person can be a satisfactory teacher without being a good scholar—they can't be a really good teacher without scholarship. This is a major research university and research capability is *first*.

The research-oriented climate of the graduate schools was therefore seen as a desirable factor in the candidates' training. Further, the hiring patterns for assistant professors confirm the theory of doctoral prestige—the inference that the status of the department where one acquires the doctorate is a predictor of the status of the department in which one will be employed. The theory was first posited by Caplow and McGee based on their 1955–57 sample, and has been repeatedly confirmed in the literature since then, as noted earlier—and always the relationship between the prestige of the Ph.D.-granting program and the prestige of the employing department had been found to be positive.

To examine the question I divided the departments in the study into

categories based on the Jones et al. (1982) rankings, as follows: Category
A departments are those ranked in the top five; Category B the next five;
Category C the next ten; and Category D are those departments ranked
below the top twenty. I applied the same categories to the assistant
professors who were appointed. The sample consists of sixty-six ranked
departments and seventy-one ranked assistant professors. Table 12
shows the distribution.

As we would expect, more A's were hired than anybody else, and the
C and D departments, which may be more upwardly mobile, had the
highest hiring rate and acquired a number of A's in the process. What is
a bit surprising in the distribution is a "trickle-down" effect that was not
uniform—that is, all of the A's and B's were not "used up" before going
to C's and D's (there was no variance by discipline in this result). If A
and B departments were combined, they would still hire less than half
the A assistant professors and slightly less than half the B's, or only 43
percent of the combined group of A and B assistant professors, while
hiring a fourth of the C's and D's.

Of course the dominance in the sample of A-ranked assistant professors does itself lend support to the doctoral prestige assumption (although we must remember that the best departments are also the largest
producers of Ph.D.'s). This kind of comment confirmed that the A's
have it:

There really was no runner-up. This person was head and shoulders above the
other candidates. He was very strong in his presentation and his credentials and
his linguistic abilities. He is a Berkeley Ph.D. Berkeley's training is outstanding.

Table 12:
Doctoral Prestige in Junior Appointments

Department Ranking	Total Appointments	Number Appointed by Ranking			
		A (1-5)	B (6-10)	C (11-20)	D (Below 20)
A (1-5)	12	5	3	1	3
B (6-10)	15	8	5	1	1
C (11-20)	24	11	6	3	4
D (Below 20)	20	7	3	3	7
Total	71	31	17	8	15

There are also some extenuating circumstances. In one instance of a D-ranked assistant professor being hired by an A-ranked department, the faculty member had actually been hired from a postdoctoral appointment at an A-ranked department. In another, the successful candidate had been engaged in clinical practice after graduate school. There were, however, no apparent modifying circumstances for any other of the D-ranked candidates selected by other than D- ranked departments, nor for the C-ranked candidates who moved up.

On the other hand, individual mentors may overshadow or replace departmental prestige. These comments were made about an A-ranked Ph.D. and one from a program not ranked:

He was in linguistics and philosophy there and was working with a very outstanding man, and so the national reputation of the department would be less relevant.

He came from a liberal arts college—but composers study with composers, not schools.

And although doctoral prestige was confirmed by the numbers as well as anecdotally as an important factor, concerns were expressed:

There are more Ph.D. producers. . . . In some sense I worry because the field is bigger and we could easily miss an Einstein—Albert wouldn't make it in today's market. We may be missing good people in smaller schools.

This doctoral prestige thing—some of it is prejudice!

Nevertheless, whatever variance exists in the prestige of appointees' institutions is not a condition forced upon the persons making the selection. These departments have been quite successful in appointing those who were their first choice; twelve instances of second choice were reported (eight were A or B candidates), and few lower on the list. But it was generally conceded that any of the top candidates would be acceptable and going to second choice was not a significant move.

We are very often making hiring decisions about people where variance in quality is 1 to 2 percent and margin of error 4 to 5 percent, so it makes very little difference whom we select out of that top group.

The match for the assistant professors in the total sample was highly positive as well; only six new appointees admitted that the job was not their first choice (see Table 13). A total proportion of 66 percent of the new appointees expressed a strong preference for the job they obtained, more than two-thirds of that group having rejected other offers. Across disciplinary divisions, the comparable proportions in the humanities

Table 13:
Attitude of New Assistant Professors toward Appointment

| | | Number of Assistant Professors | | | | |
| | | Disciplinary Division | | | Institution | |
Attitude	Total	Humanities	Social Sciences	Natural Sciences	Public	Private
Rejected other offers	33	8	15	10	18	15
Interviewed elsewhere but wanted this job	16	7	8	1	8	8
Interviewed elsewhere and wanted job elsewhere	6	1	2	3	4	2
No other interviews	19	8	8	3	9	10
Total	74	24	33	17	39	35

were 63 percent preferring, half of those rejecting other offers; in the social sciences 70 percent, with two-thirds rejecting other offers; in the natural sciences 65 percent, with nine-tenths rejecting other offers. Looked at by type of institution, there is even less variation, with the figures for public universities at 67 percent preferring, two-thirds rejecting other offers; and for private universities at 66 percent, with slightly less than two-thirds rejecting other offers.

New assistant professors were attracted to the department by diverse factors; four elements of choice were clustered at the top, two external to the institution and two internal. Most frequent mention was of the individual's professional opportunities, that is, compatibility of research interests with the strengths of the department and flexibility in teaching to permit expression of personal research interests. This included several references to interdisciplinary opportunities—an attraction for today's young scholar. In second place on the list was the matter of image—reputation and prestige of the department or the institution, e.g., "Ivy League" (again supporting the prestige theory). Third was geographical location (regardless of the location!), including reference to spouse employment in a number of instances. Image and location were summed up in this response:

This is a more prestigious place for demographic work. Primarily I felt more comfortable with the people with whom I would be working here. My family would not be happy there—it's too cold—and my wife is a freelance designer for whom there are more opportunities here than in the Midwest.

Close behind image and location was the perceived intellectual quality of the campus or department environment—"the obvious superior resources of the institution," as one woman phrased it.

The new assistant professor also recognized the value of collegiality, "fitting in":

This is my kind of department; I fit in here better. It is decentralized to the point where I can be left alone. No one is looking over your shoulder telling you how or what to teach, and this nonsupervisory mode suits me. I like teaching. I like the city. I have the freedom to explore my research interests here.

The promise of collegiality was even more of an overriding element for this advanced assistant professor:

It was really a different situation because I had been asked to come and talk at a seminar the week before, before my interview with the department was scheduled. So I came here on a Thursday and did the actual interview on Monday and Tuesday, and I got to know people a little better than I might have otherwise. I expected to come here and find people unhappy about the department, but although people were frank with me, I enjoyed their frankness and there was a

positive collegiality here. That was a bonus for me. I had a job and wasn't compelled to get one. I almost didn't come. I was pretty sure of getting tenure there and I feel the pressure more acutely here. Not that the department has higher expectations for me than I have for myself, but if I have these expectations and don't live up to them, I may give myself another chance whereas the department may not!

The personal touch mattered to some. A female humanist in the West who had rejected several other offers said:

One of the strongest selling points was how much I liked the people who interviewed me.

And a male scientist in the East, also much in demand, said:

The personal treatment I received here was impressive. I was turned off by faculty arrogance at one school.

When chairmen were asked to speculate on the reasons for an assistant professor accepting the job, the items mentioned most frequently were the same four given by the new appointees, but in slightly different order of frequency. The prestige factors and intellectual environment were thought by the chairmen to be the most important, with geographical location maintaining third place. But the most important attraction for the assistant professors—their own professional opportunities—was fourth in the chairmen's minds.

Not surprisingly, a successful chairman recognizes the competitive market, the fact that no matter how many candidates are generated by supply and demand realities or broad advertising, the top layer is still not very deep. Consequently, the department concerned with building or maintaining strength treated its applicants well. One assistant professor was impressed by "the red carpet treatment, very fine" and a chairman remarked, "I try to sell the place." Even though most disciplines operate today in a buyer's market, the more perceptive persons in those disciplines apparently understand that the definitions of an economic market with respect to supply and demand are not adequate for an academic labor market, where specific skills and qualities are being sought.

IMPACT OF APPOINTMENT

Caplow and McGee found that only 33 percent of newly appointed junior faculty members were expected by chairmen to have a long-term effect on the department. In sharp contrast in this study, chairmen reported that 83 percent of the junior appointments were expected to

have a long-run effect on the department. The chairmen responded negatively on 7 percent and hedged on 10 percent.

There were five general categories of positive response about the appointment: realization of a critical mass or stabilization of a group within the department; contributions to program development or covering specific courses; contribution of special skills, interests, or strengths; professional reputation (affecting "how we are perceived"); or simply in the vein of expecting every appointment to help build the department.

He has reinforced a group of people we have actively working. It helped to stabilize that group.

He will be the principal person in Medieval Japanese literature, crucial to the program. The senior person in this area will retire soon.

She will be making contributions by offering courses at the graduate level that we would not otherwise offer. Also, the individual matters because we have big lecture courses and everyone teaches them differently.

We see junior members as really important; they are encouraged, brought along, reviewed as necessary with a view to tenure. We obviously can't control that or even protect it—tenure is difficult at this institution, but we have never had the pattern of the Ivies. We are optimistic about the people we are bringing in.

The reasons for negative responses were split between general and specific: The department was committed to the area and the addition of a person made no difference, or it was a large department and one assistant professor did not matter much; she would leave as soon as she found something better, or his research program was weak. Several of the "uncommitted" responses involved environmental factors beyond the department's and the new appointee's control—structural reorganization, space limitations, equipment problems.

CHOOSING THE SENIOR FACULTY MEMBER

Although the ordering of the process for selecting a senior person resembles that used for the assistant professor, the character of the process is different. The senior candidate is an established professional; there is less uncertainty about potential contributions to the department and thus possibly a more confident approach by the members of the department to the task of selection. As noted earlier, the applicant pools for a senior position, especially at the full professor level, are limited.

If necessary, the search committee makes phone calls, but it was not necessary in this case. The senior person [in this department] knew everybody in the field. The committee made only one recommendation. His name just surfaced as the person we wanted to go after for this position.

The campus visit may not exist at all.

There is no visit. If it is a top person they will have been through here.

Or it may take a modified form:

The first time we talked to [the candidate] it wasn't really an interview. More, what do you think about this area, we want to beef it up, etc. He probably visited three times.

We organized a seminar series for our graduate students on research in the field and invited lots of folks, some of whom still don't know they were under consideration.

In the latter case, the person appointed remarked:

No one said there would be this job opening. I knew there would be an opening because I knew someone who had left here. The department set up a symposium, no mention of a job. It was *not subtle*.

But in a similar situation at another school, the tactic was more successfully disguised:

I gave a seminar in the department and they called me a couple of weeks later and asked me if I wanted the job. I didn't even know there was a job.

In some respects, the principles of selection may remain the same across ranks:

The committee screened on area first and then, because we wanted a full professor, on reputation and research productivity. We then ruled out people whose field was too close to those already here. We eliminated some that we knew didn't have the level of scholarship that we wanted. We eliminated some on the basis of their research interest. We would not select a person who was an excellent researcher but known to be an average teacher, and we would not select someone who wanted to come here and do only research, and that was the case in one instance. Everyone in our department is expected to teach graduates and undergraduates.

We had a high-flying senior person come in one year. He asked the graduate students if they were going to be voting on his appointment and when they said no, he said he would be wasting time on them. We didn't hire him.

The senior candidate is likely to be wooed at a higher pitch than the junior candidate, and the visit includes a broader cast of characters on the campus. Following are reports from four different universities:

The visit was primarily the same [as that of the assistant professor also appointed] except that we were trying to sell ourselves to him a little bit more than he was trying to sell himself to us. Also, he interviewed with the dean and provost.

They [the senior candidates] talked with senior faculty in related departments and to deans and the vice president.

On the visit the candidate gives a talk, the faculty "attends" them, they are "feted."

The interview was the same [as for the junior position filled] except that the two finalists interviewed with the provost and the president.

Both successes and disappointments in the courtships were recounted, as in these examples from the same university:

Our timing was good. He wanted to be a senior scholar with a reduction of responsibility.

Our first offer was to a person from Indiana who got a counteroffer from there and stayed.

The reasons for the choice of the particular senior appointee were not articulated as well by chairmen as they had been for the assistant professors. There was much mention of research quality and significance, and there seemed to be a desire for breadth:

I think it was that he was more mature in the field and his interests were broader. He does a lot of collaborative work.

He brought greater breadth. His work is more theoretical. He is able to evolve and synthesize.

He represented an area the department didn't have.

Personality was mentioned—again, fitting into the department. "Everyone knew after meeting him that he would be a good team member." It may be that this is an even more important factor for the senior than for the junior appointment, in the sense of ensuring that the faculty is comfortable with the prospective appointee. The senior person may be more of a professional threat; as one chairman acknowledged, "I brought him down for a lecture and the department got very nervous." Also on the subject of "matching," another said about a new associate professor:

Ostensibly, her work is good and she is younger than the other candidate and therefore thought to have more potential. But really we just liked her personally a lot better than we liked him.

Some remarks were surprisingly similar to those made about assistant professors:

His research record and reputation [were the basis for the choice]. We assess teaching ability but it is largely secondary, but we would not hire a lousy teacher. We have no place to hide someone like that. Everyone in our department teaches undergraduates.

Research is all important. Teaching counts some. Being a good guy around the department counts a smidgen.

Finally, and perhaps most accurately, several chairmen simply admitted that intuition played a large part in the selection process.

For the senior person, the prestige of the department from which he or she was recruited played a lesser role in the selection decision than did the Ph.D. departments of the assistant professors. The same methodology was used, when applied to hiring department and previous job, as that described earlier for hiring department and Ph.D. source of assistant professors. Table 14 shows the distribution of senior appointments in the twenty-eight ranked departments.

Note that the sample included thirteen appointees who were not ranked. In recruitments from foreign universities, we enjoyed the benefit of the "brain drain" from the U.K. Another émigré, who had spent a year at another school in the United States before moving to the job in this study, remarked: "The quality of life is better in Europe, but the science is better here."

In this group of successful candidates, all but five had been the first choice of the department; the five were two full professors and three associate professors. As might be expected, all of the senior appointees interviewed were at their first-choice job, although one woman who had moved because her husband lost his job remarked that she would have preferred to stay where she was. Four of the associate professors (out of fourteen respondents) and ten of the full professors (out of twenty-one respondents) either applied or were nominated only to that single position or were personally recruited by the department, that is, they were not "on the market." Seven of the associate professors and nine of the full professors had rejected opportunities to be considered elsewhere.

The new senior faculty members were attracted to the department for diverse reasons, ordered differently by academic rank. Professors gave the most mention to the reputation of the department—often indicating potential rather than present prestige, a desire to lead or to be involved in building or creating. A distant second on their list were salary and perquisites, tied with and sometimes overlapping research support (resources and emphasis). Third came quality of students, particularly the graduate students and graduate program, along with richness of the

Table 14:
Prestige of Department in Senior Appointments

Department Ranking	Total Appointments	Number Appointed by Ranking				
		A (1-5)	B (6-10)	C (11-20)	D (Below 20)	Other*
A (1-5)	5	2	1	1	-	1
B (6-10)	3	3	-	-	-	-
C (11-20)	12	2	1	1	2	6
D (Below 20)	14	1	2	1	4	6
Total	34	8	4	3	6	13

*Detail of "Other" column:

A   1 Foreign university

C   2 Foreign university
    2 Research institute
    1 Industry (research)
    1 Liberal arts college

D   3 Foreign university
    1 Private practice
    1 Liberal arts college
    1 Unemployed

campus and/or community environment. These were typical of responses, from widely separated geographical locations and a public and
a private university:

I'm a native of the state, but that's minor; my wife and I have family here, but
she was not excited about moving back. You really don't move for the money,
although I got an increase in pay. It's just a generally good department, getting
better. I have nice new offices; they spent over one and a half million dollars on
computing equipment, of which I am the primary user. They provided support
for the postdoc I brought with me. I got to approve all the architects' drawings
for the renovations.

Mainly we wanted to go east. Secondarily we wanted a city with a first-rate
orchestra. My wife and I are both elitist and we want our kids in good schools
and we were able to achieve that here. We live in a nice neighborhood just a few
blocks from the campus. Professionally, I wanted an environment where the arts
and sciences are strong. Although my department [in the natural sciences] is not
ranked very high yet, there are several arts and sciences departments that have
excellent ratings.

Associate professors, like assistant professors, were attracted to the department by compatibility with their research interests, and by intellectually stimulating colleagues. Second was the department's reputation. Both attractions are reflected in this response:

In industry my salary and benefits were much higher. It was a totally different function. I did no teaching there and the research orientation was different. The move involved giving up short-term things to gain long-term things. This probably is one of the few chemistry departments that number one, already has some initial research in the areas I'm interested in and number two, is willing to take a chance on the future importance of the research area. I think they are very foresighted.

For these new appointees there were also "push" factors—reasons for leaving their previous department; but the "pull" was expressed more strongly and a few said there were no push factors at all. At the top of the professors' list was a feeling of having done what they wanted to do there: "It was time to leave." Their second-place motivator was quality of life—wanting to leave the city in order to enjoy the peace and quiet of a settled community, or wanting to leave the small town in order to enjoy the greater cultural opportunities of the urban life. Associate professors had left because their department was unwilling to tenure or slow to promote, or because they felt their future limited in other ways (for example, by conflict with senior colleagues), or as in the case noted above, for professional fulfillment—"giving up short-term things to gain long-term things."

The opinions of the chairmen about the attraction for professors, contrary to self-aggrandizement notions, gave highest points to the campus and community environment ("this is a nice place to live"), with department reputation coming far down the list and research support below that; salary and perquisites were mentioned only once and quality of students not at all. They showed slightly more rapport with associate professors by echoing their top reason of research interests, but neither the associate professors' choices of department reputation nor of colleagues was high on the list.

As for push factors, the chairmen's most frequent response was "none" or "I don't know." For professors, they thought that geographical location, including opportunities for spouse employment, was an important negative point in the previous appointment. Again, the chairmen were more sensitive to the associate professors, identifying tenure chances and related issues as the primary reason for leaving.

The fact that chairmen often err in identifying the most important factors in a career decision suggests a lack of comprehension on the part of academic leaders as to what pulls or pushes a faculty member to or from the academic position.

Generally, the selection of associate professors and full professors ranged from a process quite similar to that used for assistant professors to the personal recruitment of a distinguished faculty member. Except in the case of the very junior associate professors who had not been tenured at their previous positions, the causes of variance in the process are difficult to identify. The variation seems to have more connection with departmental personality—how the department views itself and its needs—than with any other condition.

OFFER AND ACCEPTANCE

The end of the recruiting story is much like the beginning, but differs at the level of participation in decisionmaking from the era chronicled by Caplow and McGee—less change than intensification of the democratic process. In their late 1950s sample, all members of the department participated in the hiring process in only 31 percent of the hiring departments, and the chairman exercised sole authority in 13 percent of the departments. In this study, the ninety-one recruiting departments made their hiring decisions at the levels shown in Table 15. As in the earlier table on the origination of the position, there is a slight tendency toward committee decision in public universities, in the natural sciences, and in larger departments. In 82 percent of the departments, however, the decisions were made by the full faculty. No decisions were made by the chairman acting alone.

This pattern presents an even higher rate of participation in the department for the appointment decision than existed for definition of the position to be filled, and conflicts with an oligarchic representation made by researchers in the 1970s. Touraine (1974) commented that decisions about faculty appointments were made by the chairman and senior members of the department. Kenen and Kenen (1978), working with Parsons and Platt's earlier unpublished data and examining perceptions of power among the faculty, concluded that department chairmen and senior faculty were perceived to have the major control over faculty appointments. Using later data, though, Baldridge et al. (1978) and Smelser and Content (1980) saw decisionmaking more broadly based in the department, as confirmed by this study.

That the process has become more participatory may reflect societal trends away from authoritarian behavior in organizations. Clark (1987), however, points out that ideas and devices such as "rank-and-file 'participation' and 'quality circles,' which American business firms have explored in the 1970s and 1980s to increase production by spreading responsibility and decision making, have been operative in universities for a long time" and illustrates his position with a quote from one of his respondents:

Authority is delegated down to the people who really have to live with the results of the decision. As a consequence, the faculty doesn't feel that it is being put upon; we feel that we made the decision we have to live with, and it is really very successful. (p. 156)

Broadening the base further is the addition at this point, not mentioned by either Caplow and McGee or later researchers, of graduate student involvement in the appointment decision, probably deriving from student demands in the late 1960s for a voice in governance. Graduate students participated in an advisory capacity in more than half of the departments surveyed: "The graduate students are a very important part of our department; they have a voice in everything."

The more comprehensive decisionmaking did not seem to result in dilution of effect. For example, care was taken by some departments to ensure that an informed decision was being made. Following are comments about decisions on a full professor, an associate professor, and an assistant professor.

Table 15:
Decision Level of Faculty Selection

Unit of Comparison	Number of Departments Decision Level		
	Full Faculty	Committee	Total
Institution:			
Public	41*	12	53
Private	34*	4	38
Total	75	16	91
Disciplinary Division:			
Humanities	28*	4	32
Social Sciences	25*	3	28
Natural Sciences	22	9	31
Total	75	16	91
Department Size:			
Small	27	4	31
Medium	37*	6	17
Large	11*	6	43
Total	75	16	91

*For two associate professor appointments in large social sciences departments in public universities and for one full professor appointment in a medium-sized social sciences department in a private university, the decision was made by a committee consisting of the tenured faculty in the department. Decisions in the same departments concerning assistant professors were made by the full faculty.

We send a form about each candidate to the faculty asking questions so that it is not just a yes or no ballot.

A form is sent to the department members on which they make written comments and particularly note what contact they have had with the candidate and indicate what their decision would be about making an offer. Then the faculty meets to discuss.

The department members who have met the candidate fill out a ballot. It is not just yes and no but comments about teaching, research potential, etc.

All this democracy ensures that the departmental decision is not made without controversy! Reports from two universities follow:

There were a few dissents initially, but it was finally unanimous.

The faculty and research associate and graduate student representatives meet and then there is a free-for-all.

But the conscientious chairman works to bring the department together:

I try to bring the department to consensus on an appointment. The department should be in a position of welcoming a newcomer, nurturing our younger people.

This kind of recognition of the human relations factor is a marked departure from the tone of the Caplow and McGee interviews. Two other quotes from participants in the current study support the new attitude:

This is a nice department to live in. Our department meetings can be hot and heavy but we reach unanimity, we have mutual respect, courtesy, reasonableness. What we are ultimately hiring is a person.

I think we were able to hire her because we made a great personal effort.

After the department members reached agreement, bloodily or otherwise, the actual offer required administrative approval. Frustration often ensued for candidates, like these two assistant professors at a public and a private university:

This was the job I really wanted, but getting it was tough! I had an offer from Illinois that I was going to accept, and I called them from New York and told them about the offer. They called an emergency meeting. I tried to call the chairman at the time that I was supposed to call her, and her line was busy for nine hours! I finally got her and she told me that they wanted to offer me the job but the university hadn't cleared it yet. This was in February. I told Illinois that I was waiting to hear about this job and could not accept theirs. A couple of months later, Illinois called and told me that they had not found anyone for the job yet and asked me if I would be interested. Toronto called and then offered

me a job at the interview. I kept calling here. I finally got appointed in October. Things are great now, but I still feel angry about what went on.

The circumstances of the offer were ambiguous. They told me they were pretty sure it was going to be me, but they had to wait for the central committee to act and I shouldn't turn down anything I wanted. I came here looking for housing and was told that they were sorry, they still couldn't be definite. It was two months after the interview before I got the first phone call. It took almost four months after that for the process. I was not thrilled about the school as a result.

Five of the universities required review and approval of *tenured* appointments by central faculty committees who were advisory to the dean or provost, an understandable procedure. But at two of the institutions, one public and one private, requests to make an appointment at the assistant professor level were also referred to central committees, whereas at the other four schools the chairmen sent their requests to appoint an assistant professor direct to the dean and usually received approval to make the formal offer within a few days. The review at the junior level was viewed as unnecessarily prolonging the process and was deemed a nuisance by the chairmen. One remarked rather sarcastically: "When I see the white smoke coming out of the administration building chimney, I write the offer letter." No rejections by the administration were reported at the junior level in either of the central-review institutions, which raises a question as to whether the procedure is desirable at the junior level. We recall Caplow and McGee's Recommendation No. 9 calling for "regular, orderly procedures" for faculty selection, and remarking that the "development of new committees and functionaries to diffuse the responsibility for appointments is almost wholly undesirable," often leading to rubber-stamp behavior (*Marketplace*, pp. 249–250).

Prior to, during, and after administrative referral, negotiation became a factor in the appointment. Negotiation by the chairmen took place on two levels, sometimes simultaneously—with the dean and with the candidate. Items of negotiation with the dean ran to inclusion of the new faculty member in special programs such as summer and research support and housing, start-up funds for research, and salary. As to the last, one respondent explained:

The faculty votes and I then phone up the dean and we argue about the salary involved. It's a ritual. There is a script for it. He points out that our assistant professors earn more than anyone else in Arts and Sciences, and I tell him that I won't make any offer unless I can make a good one. This all takes only a day or two beyond the time of the faculty vote.

Research support could be a stickier issue, as reported by this chairman:

I recommend to the Dean of Arts and Sciences; it takes about a week to get the draft offer letter with salary approved. But if the Dean of Research says there is no money, he effectively vetoes the offer. This veto has been exercised at times. The Dean of Research is very confident in his own opinions. But more typically, I talk with the Dean [of Research] and try to generate funds. He wants to know what the department can contribute, and we get a package together.

Negotiation with the candidate may have covered such additional items as moving expenses, laboratory or office space, and teaching assignment. The chairmen reported negotiation in about 40 percent of the appointments, about two-thirds of that figure with candidates and the remaining third with the administration. Incidence of negotiation escalated with rank and involved almost all of the full professors; today's senior candidates appear to be writing their own tickets. We could surmise that with a "lost generation" of scholars in the 1970s, research universities today are competing for a smaller pool of seasoned scholars, having failed to develop their own faculties. Two senior scholars alluded to their experience:

The original offer was unacceptable and it took about nine months longer to iron everything out. I sent them seven single-spaced pages. I like to have everything in writing. I particularly was negotiating for a computer.

I negotiated quite a bit. All the basics, to get me to a position where I felt that the trade-offs in coming here balanced. The salary was of less concern than the optional needs, the research needs.

There was, as might be expected, less negotiation at the junior level. The chairmen reported negotiation with only twenty-four assistant professors. Among the seventy-four assistant professor respondents (a smaller sample than the ninety-six on which the chairmen were reporting because not all ninety-six could be contacted), negotiation or lack of it was distributed as shown in Table 16, with almost an even split between negotiators and nonnegotiators. The only differences by sex in the study occurred here, where the proportion of women who negotiated the conditions of their appointment was much lower than that of the men—56 percent of the men negotiated their terms of employment but only 29 percent of the women did so. Further, the fledgling natural scientists, who of course were likely to have laboratory needs, appeared to be the most likely to negotiate—at 76 percent of their total as compared to 45 percent of the total social scientists and 29 percent of humanists. There is also a difference between public and private institutions, with 57 percent of the new assistant professors in private universities negotiating and only 38 percent of those in public universities doing so.

Table 16:
Negotiation of Employment Contract by Assistant Professors

	Number of Assistant Professors		
	Did Negotiate	Did Not Negotiate	Total
Institution:			
Public	15	24	39
Private	20	15	35
Total	35	39	74
Disciplinary Division:			
Humanities	7	17	24
Social Sciences	15	18	33
Natural Sciences	13	4	17
Total	35	39	74
Sex:			
Male	28	22	50
Female	7	17	24
Total	35	39	74

This junior group reported some incidence of specific negotiation over spouse employment, as by this physicist in a state university:

My wife is also an academic and we had a hard time finding jobs we both liked in the same city. I had been on the East Coast and she had been in the Midwest, and we decided that had to stop. The main thing we were concerned with in negotiation was exactly what her position was and how stable that would be. The dean really created a position for her and she is now on the tenure track.

Note also these departures from the traditional in the appointments of an advanced assistant professor and an untenured associate professor (half of an academic couple), both women:

She negotiated moving expenses—she has a husband and five children—and although we couldn't get that from the college, we had some money available from a department fund and were able to give her that and summer support as well.

I wanted to be clear about exactly what my position was: The unanimity of the department's position plus a letter from the dean spelling out what was considered to be acceptable in the way of publications for tenure. I received a salary increase over my last job, but I gave up a 5 percent mortgage there and negotiated more money to make up for that. I also negotiated paid leave time.

Many assistant professors of both sexes expressed regret at not having negotiated before accepting the position; one female humanist said

ruefully, "I'm really stupid about that—had I but known!" A male social scientist capped his complaint, on a warm day in April, with, " and I wish I had negotiated an air conditioner for this office!" A male geologist was particularly distressed:

I didn't negotiate because I was naive. In retrospect, it really hurt me. It has taken me two years to get a laboratory set up. I needed $20,000 worth of equipment; eventually it got worked out.

Those who did negotiate frequently mentioned that they had been advised to do so by someone in their graduate department or a junior faculty member in the hiring department: A favorite object of their negotiations was a personal computer!

These data on negotiation contain numerous disparities between respondent groups. For example, note this chairman's remark: "She negotiated salary—she was a faculty brat and knew about those things!" The appointee in question indicated no negotiation. It appears that these differences occurred through lapse of memory on the chairman's part about a junior appointment; details seemed much more firmly fixed in the case of senior recruitment. Another factor that may have influenced the disparity was chairman rotation. A new chairman may have been quite interested and involved in a senior appointment as a member of the department, but less interested and consequently less informed about the closing details of junior recruitment.

SPECIAL CASES

A word at this point about special cases that might be considered negotiated positions, as compared to positions acquired through open competition. Inasmuch as these special situations constitute 8 percent of the appointments in the sample and, judging from anecdotal information, are representative, they are worth a brief mention.

The eleven special cases in this sample illustrate exceptions in today's recruiting picture: the mom and pop shop; the star attraction; the supporting cast; and going home again. The first of these is the position or positions created for a couple (usually married but not always), at least one of whom the department wants very badly. Recruitment is normally a word-of-mouth arrangement; people "let it be known" that they are available. Variations are the split position for two well qualified juniors, or the non-tenure-track position or staff job created for the half of the couple for whom it is the best solution in the current circumstances. When the couple is housed in the same department, it is a very delicate situation, about which department members talk in circumspect tones. If either mom or pop is in some other department, the couple's accommodation is treated much more matter-of-factly.

The second situation needs little explanation. The "star"—a distin-

guished professor at some other institution—is lured to the university in order to double (at least) the prestige of the department in which he, or sometimes even she, lands.

And of course the supporting cast is necessary in order to make a newly recruited distinguished member of the faculty feel more comfortable in his new and strange surroundings. This is accomplished by permitting him to attract new people who are more like him than any of the incumbent faculty members are likely to be, and creating faculty positions into which he can move such people. He brings in his candidates and the department votes them through. Departmental reaction is mixed—some enthusiasm, some cynicism.

The last scenario is a modified version of silver-cording, where the former student has gone out into the cruel world and found it not quite as hospitable as had been expected, and wants to return "home" to alma mater. The alumnus or alumna who goes home again may compete for the position; but sometimes, as were the cases in this sample, he or she slides into the position via a temporary position and becomes a safe choice when a tenure-track opening occurs. Here the department members are usually relieved that they did not have the burden of a search with its element of uncertainty, although some of course wonder what good person they did not get, especially in retrospect.

We probably won't do it again. We were comfortable with her and she was an adequate teacher and it saved us some trouble, but we may have done ourselves a disservice. Did we miss someone very good?

A FOOTNOTE

A senior professor in the social sciences at one state university said this:

You should say somewhere in your book: Faculty by nature have very big egos—the fact that you have to get up in front of a classroom and perform takes a little bit of being extroverted. Our departed faculty member had an overblown sense of his own value and worth, but perhaps we all do. We have to think we are good or we can't function very well.

It may be that this confidence in one's ability to perform is a deciding factor, more often than not, in the choices made among finalists. It is not only what others think of the candidate, but what the candidate thinks of himself or herself. The senior professor's opinion is reflected in these two remarks from new appointees, the first from an assistant professor of economics and the second from a professor of English:

I was interviewed by three faculty members at the AEA for about forty to forty-five minutes. When I visited campus I gave a seminar, spent the whole day with

various members of the faculty, had lunch and dinner with faculty members. It takes selling yourself—I'm good at that.

They made me a full professor and gave me a 66 percent raise. They got a job for my wife and worked out a mortgage plan for me so that we could buy a $200,000 house that we wanted. I'm very good. I've written six books and have been nominated for the Pulitzer.

5

Observations on Separation

I think his main reason for going there was that they seemed
real pleased to have him work for them.

ASSOCIATE PROFESSOR OF ECONOMICS

Thus far, the respondents in the study have described a highly conscientious process of search and selection in staffing the academic department. We have seen that department members spend a large number of hours and dollars in filling a faculty position. In this chapter, the process of separation from the department is considered—when the careful recruiting effort fails to secure a faculty member who proves tenurable, or who moves on voluntarily; and when the association lasts and phases into the retirement years.

The stage is set by two sets of numbers: First, Table 17 compares appointments with terminations in the current data. There are two points here that confirm notions of the changes that have occurred in resource allocation affecting staffing within the institution: (1) The full professors were not replaced in kind, and (2) the shift to the natural sciences recognized earlier in comparisons between the 1958 and 1986 appointment data occurred *within* the current study as well. Although full professors accounted for sixty of the terminations, at about 36 percent of the sample, they numbered only twenty-four in appointments, or about 18 percent of the sample. In similar fashion, there were forty terminations in the natural sciences, 24 percent, and forty-five appointments, 33 percent. Both the humanities and social sciences lost ground, with terminations at approximately 38 percent each and appointments at 31 percent for the humanities and 36 percent for the social sciences.

The replacement rate was considerably higher in the current study, probably reflecting a greater availability of qualified candidates. Caplow and McGee's data showed 143 vacancies with ninety one appointments, or a 64 percent replacement; the current data showed 167 terminations and 137 appointments, or an 82 percent replacement.

The second comparison that is useful in describing the character of academic mobility is shown in Table 18, dealing with type of termina-

Table 17:
Terminations and Appointments

	Terminations 1983-84		Appointments 1984-85	
	No.	%	No.	%
Academic Rank:				
Assistant Professor	87	52.1	96	70.1
Associate Professor	20	12.0	17	12.4
Professor	60	35.9	24	17.5
Total	167	100.0	137	100.0
Disciplinary Division:				
Humanities	63	37.7	43	31.4
Social Sciences	64	38.3	49	35.8
Natural Sciences	40	24.0	45	32.8
Total	167	100.0	137	100.0

tion. Retirements have increased substantially from 17 percent of the Caplow and McGee sample to 23 percent of the current sample. Concomitantly, loss of faculty members through death has dropped from 11 percent of the 1958 total termination figure to 3 percent in the current study. But the incidence of dismissal and resignation in the 1958 and the 1986 data is about the same, noteworthy amidst talk of higher standards and greater difficulty in achieving tenure, and of market conditions that would be thought to hinder mobility.

Table 18:
Terminations, by Type

Type of Termination	1958 Study		1986 Study	
	No.	%	No.	%
Dismissal	35	24.5	43	25.7
Resignation	67	46.9	81	48.5
Retirement	25	17.4	38	22.8
Death	16	11.2	5	3.0
Total	143	100.0	167	100.0

DISMISSAL

Perhaps the most surprising nonchange is the stability of proportions in dismissal and resignation, in spite of the change in market structure. Contrary to academic myth, there is little difference in the toll taken by tenure denials. Although there is a widespread feeling in academia that it is much tougher to achieve tenure today, the suspicion is not supported by the facts (in a relative sense—there may in truth be higher standards that the same proportion of assistant professors is meeting).

Dismissal of the assistant professor, that is (in this sample), denial of tenure or denial of reappointment prior to tenure consideration, accounts for only a quarter of the terminations from academic positions. Dismissal, however, could be considered an important indicator of the effectiveness of the selection process. If we assume a fairly constant rate of appointment since 1978 (the date when most of these departing assistant professors were appointed) and compare the incidence of dismissal (43) with the incidence of junior appointment in the sample (97), it could be suggested that the selection process is not a good predictor of success on the job. Even allowing for a greater number of appointments in 1978, say 150, the failure rate shakes one's confidence in the system. What went wrong? An examination of the cases of dismissal may provide some clues.

The Central Committee

First, it might be suspected that an initial complication occurs in the tenuring process by the split responsibility, between the academic department and a central faculty committee that is advisory to the provost. Generally, the academic department, in this sample, could make the decision to deny tenure; an exception was one campus where all decisions were required to be sent forward to the review committee. In all cases, if the department reached a favorable decision, a recommendation for tenure was sent to the committee.

In the dismissals in this study, however, the denial decision occurred at the departmental level in more than two-thirds of the cases (see Table 19)—at 70 percent, this is slightly higher than the 1958 proportion of 67 percent. In the two universities where most of the actions took place, Private E and Public F, there is a clear difference, with about half of the decisions made by a central committee in Private E and less than a fifth made centrally in Public F. It can also be observed that the congruence between departmental and institutional standards lessens as the ranked quality of the department decreases. Or, put another way, there is dissonance in the organization.

Examples of dissonance may also be drawn from these comments, the first from a chairman and the second from a colleague:

We felt that there had been unethical behavior on the part of the committee. I personally requested an opportunity to meet with the committee and debate their decision, but they would not do that. It would be normal that they would not meet with the department representative and I did not really expect them to accept my challenge. The dean did not support tenure for our candidate.

We put him up for promotion and the first decision came down in April. We appealed, thought at first that the appeal might go someplace. He *is* a philosopher, does not just spout philosophic theory. He was philosophic in his life, sensitive, judicious, wise. His values were attached to his feet, not just words. We didn't know finally until somewhat late. We might have made more public efforts if we had known. Perhaps we were led on.

And the disagreement in values may fester among the faculty, as noted by this chairman:

He is used by the department as an example of poor administrative judgment: " . . . *and* they didn't give Smith tenure!"

Table 19:
Decision Level of Tenure Denial

Unit of Comparison	Number of Decisions		
	Department	Central Committee	Total
Institution:			
University A (Public)	2	-	2
University B (Private)	1	-	1
University C (Public)	3	1	4
University D (Private)	2	3	5
University E (Private)	8	7	15
University F (Public)	13	3	16
Total	29	14	43
Department Ranking*:			
1 to 5	-	-	-
6 to 10	7	1	8
11 to 20	11	4	15
Below 20	8	4	12
Total	26	9	35

*Ranking used is the faculty quality factor from Jones et al. (1982). Only ranked disciplines are included above; 8 departments in the total (43) were in disciplines not ranked.

On the other hand, it was not unknown for an academic department to shirk its responsibility, both in counseling and evaluation:

The department made a serious effort to keep him. He was hired on soft money, I believe, through the Center, and his connection with the department was tenuous. As a teacher he was a disaster; students complained about him. He covered medical, intellectual, and demographic aspects in his work and he was out of his depth. There were intellectual problems with his work, flaws that were known to the department—but they bucked it on up to the central administration to deal with.

Then too, of course, there is the argument that humanists on central committees cannot adequately judge the work of natural or social scientists, and vice versa:

The variety of personnel on the review committee results in various degrees of stringency being applied. There is too much emphasis on quantitative factors and a lot of poor publishing results, strung out, duplicative. There are hard sciences attitudes that are now being applied. The idea of going beyond a certain point in scholarship doesn't mean anything in the humanities. Concepts such as "cutting edge" and "breakthrough" don't apply. If there is a cutting edge, it cuts in a circle.

It must be stressed, however, that the majority of the dismissals in the sample were *not* central decisions but rather departmental.

Assistant Professor's Interests

Second, where the denial of tenure or reappointment occurred at the departmental level, and although candidate and hiring department agreed on the importance of research at the outset, there may have been a divergence of interest on the new assistant professor's part as time passed after appointment. All of the tenure or reappointment denials were said to be based on scholarship—the research and publication criterion on which the assistant professors were evaluated for selection. Colleagues of the departed faculty members had candid comments about shortcomings in scholarship:

He was strongly at odds with the administration as to what criteria should be applied to a faculty member. He won the teaching award two years in a row. He was very helpful and popular with other faculty members about helping with their research, but his own research program was in trouble. In part he was having trouble because he was spending so much time working with students and other faculty on their own research problems. A lot of people with a higher profile will have acknowledgments in their papers to him because he was able to solve a problem that they couldn't. We had a lot of arguments. I told him that he

was removing himself from a system that he couldn't beat and that the students would lose. He is not very tolerant of imperfections in a bureaucracy. He spends a lot of energy banging his head against the administration building and you just get a bloody head that way. I agreed with his principles but you have to face the real world.

He was a good friend of mine, very smart, but not interested in playing the academic game. The letters in his file were negative, people didn't know him. I tried to encourage him to establish visibility. I suggested getting in touch with [a prominent younger person at another university] as a link. I tried to convince him he had to publish, criticize other people's work, etc. I also think he developed a psychological mechanism of not putting forth one hundred percent effort, as very bright people sometimes do.

He just didn't publish. He came up for tenure with only two articles of very limited focus. He had been reworking his dissertation and hadn't had it accepted for publication but actually refused to show it to the department. We had no choice.

Failure in Collegiality

Third, along with or possibly affecting perceptions of a weakness in scholarly quality, the assistant professor may have failed to deliver on the promise of colleagueship, or the department may have failed to provide a supportive environment, as indicated by these comments:

There was a split vote in the department that is very rare, not reflecting spectacularly strong views, facts, but rather a division within the hearts of many people. This was a man in whose corner almost everyone was—he was extremely bright, had good ideas but couldn't get them down on paper. Almost everyone in the department had Dutch uncle talks with him.

The department was not at ease with the decision of her being turned down for reappointment. She was surprised, shocked. She had been given signals by some senior faculty contrary to the feelings of others. There was egregious miscommunication on the part of certain senior faculty members.

It is a department's responsibility to make as clear as possible any points that emerged from evaluations or discussions or whatever, to warn well in advance if you can. Everyone is busy—the teaching looked okay; in the fourth or fifth year I would have yelled loudly if I had noticed earlier, but what happens again and again is that the members of the department read much more thoroughly the last two years. Teaching is more visible than the research.

Change in Standards

Finally, and perhaps most disastrous for the selection process, the standards may have changed between the time of appointment and the time of tenure consideration, as in these two cases, the first a committee

decision in University E and the second a department decision in University F:

I thought the committee made a very narrow decision in his case. That year they decided to adopt an extremely rigid set of criteria. He was turned down on the basis of not having a book although he had several articles.

This is an upwardly mobile department. We are targeting being in the top five. We have to hire better people than we have.

An interesting revelation in these dismissal data is that the departments ranked in the top ten accounted for only eight of the dismissals, and there were none among the top five. The chairmen of three top-five departments had these remarks about their lack of termination activity:

We hire carefully, do not make it impossible for young people. They know if they continue to do well they will be tenured.

There is no problem here, no quotas, no problem such as exists at Harvard and Yale. I think this a better way to do it, our way, it builds departments.

This is a very stable department. In twenty-four years no one has left this department except a European who wanted to go home and a guy who went back East.

This suggests that the department that is less sure of its own quality, or more anxious to improve it, may be unable or unwilling to provide the assistant professor with the intellectual and supportive environment required for success. In some instances, too, there may not be universally shared values among the faculty of the institution, resulting in central decisions varying from those made at the departmental level. At any rate, the failure of the selection process to predict tenurability may be not so much a fault of the procedure itself as in its application, especially in the variance between criteria used for selection and criteria used for the tenure decision.

Discussion of dismissal frequently led to discussion of the tenure system, for which there were mixed reviews. The first two comments below were made by senior professors in the same natural sciences department; the third came from an untenured assistant professor of psychology:

The tenure system has come home to roost—it is damaging to the people that it is designed to protect. Up or out is *bad*! Term appointments or extension of probation or other possibilities need to be explored. I think tenure is a disaster.

I thought he deserved tenure, but even though he did not get tenure, it is bad that he had to leave anyway. It is more of a disadvantage than an advantage for those of us that are in fields with ties to business, industry and government

outside the university. About ten years ago we considered doing away with tenure here, but people who don't have outside ties cling to it—for example, people in the humanities.

The tenure system has one advantage. It is a goad for people to get going and be productive early. The disadvantages are a social fractionation within the department. There is a removal of motivational support and the promotion of dead wood behavior post-tenure. There is overproduction of questionable research. In my opinion granting tenure for life is a mistake; long-term renewable contracts are preferable.

Beyond these opinions, there is the cynical shrug from a tenured associate professor:

Of course people in the academic world don't make academic assessments. They operate on signals from publishers, etcetera.

In several fields, there seemed to be a tension between "basic" and "applied" research that created problems in the tenure process:

The field of physical education suffers, is suspect, because of the body-mind Medieval bifurcation. Our faculty does clinical kinds of things, and that affects the way administrators look at physical education and where they want to put departments of physical education. People in applied research are finding it increasingly difficult to get tenure. This is a problem that we have to solve—we need to do a better job of educating colleagues in other disciplines about this.

Finally, we have this chairman's wry defense of a department's efforts to provide collegial support for the junior faculty member:

We review annually with special attention to assistant professors, and then there is a formal third-year review for the junior faculty. I go in and ask them about their publications and so forth. We have a mentor system here; one person volunteers to keep up with each new assistant professor. (Of course I don't know whether the assistant professors know they have mentors!)

RESIGNATION

A statistic almost as surprising as the lack of change in tenure denials is the representation of voluntary resignation in the sample. The proportion of resignations attests to a continuing degree of mobility, across ranks, that might not be expected in today's market.

Generally, Caplow and McGee's motives for migration—prestige, security, and authority—have been modified over the years into a more personal mold of status and professional concerns, that is, a personal career framework. There is not as much contradiction in the reasons for leaving and the attractions of the new position as occurred in the earlier

study, where reasons for leaving were seen as personal and attraction as professional. Perceived attractions of the new job at the assistant professor level and the reasons new appointees gave for selecting a job are also similar, centering on research interests. Throughout, the 1958 motivators of prestige, security, and authority are less prominent. Today we might say that motives for migration are more accurately described as quality of life and professional fulfillment.

"Push" Factors

In this continuing mobility, an obvious question concerning resignations of assistant professors is whether tenure pressures had anything to do with the departure. In this sample the answer was yes in slightly more than a third of the cases, as shown in the breakdown of number of resignations of assistant professors affected by tenure concerns (see Table 20). The same two institutions, one private and one public, that accounted for the majority of the involuntary terminations of assistant professors also accounted for the greatest number of voluntary resignations among that group. Note, however, that in seventeen out of the twenty three cases in these two schools, tenure was not an issue. Notice also that quality of department, as in tenure denial, appears to have little

Table 20:
Tenure Stress in Assistant Professor Resignations

	Number of Assistant Professors		
	Tenure Stress Cited	Tenure Stress Not Cited	Total
Institution:			
Public A	3	1	4
Private B	3	4	7
Public C	2	3	5
Private D	1	1	2
Private E	5	7	12
Public F	1	10	11
Total	15	26	41
Department Ranking:			
1-5	1	-	1
6-10	5	2	7
11-20	3	11	14
Below 20	2	8	10
Not ranked	4	5	9
Total	15	26	41

effect on tenure concerns, but the greater number of voluntary resignations of assistant professors was from the lower-ranked departments.
   These comments by colleagues provided insights into tenure fears:

It was just a question of whether he would leave prior to being denied tenure.
He was a Chicago Ph.D. and had extremely high expectations regarding the
quality of his written work. In graduate school he was instilled with these high
expectations of scholarly work and felt his papers were never quite at the level
he expected of himself. In my opinion, what he never really realized was that for
every published paper there are a number of rejections and part of the process is
responding to criticism. He may have had some inability to deal with rejection.
He is a very good economist. Also, it might have been better if he'd had someone senior in his field to work with who would have kind of forced him to
submit his work. Fortunately when I was in his position I did have someone
senior to work with. Watching him go through these first few years of an
academic career makes me think that it is a mistake to hire good junior people in
a field where there are no senior people. There is a kind of intellectual isolation.

Her leaving was something of a surprise. She waived review for tenure. At her
previous university she was very close to a man in the late stages of assistant
professor who got so nervous during his tenure review that his ulcer hemor-
rhaged and he died! She also had a bad experience on her book. Some of the
people who originally liked it thought she had destroyed it after she revised it to
a more theoretical viewpoint. Everyone here talked with her and encouraged her
to seek tenure.

Themes of apprehension for the young scholar were woven into these
responses: intellectual isolation and intellectual incompatibility with
senior colleagues, along with, in these two cases, graduate training that
produces unrealistic expectations and the "horror stories" surrounding
the tenure process.
   Some similar thoughts about intellectual climate are expressed by colleagues of those assistant professors who had no concerns about tenure
when they left:

He was discouraged by the profession, which is controlled by senior traditional-
ists. He is extremely talented and well schooled in his particular area, but he was
up against a wall here.

There was personal tension between him and the local star in his field.

He had to commute to [a scientific laboratory several hundred miles away] to do
research.

Another problem is that there really aren't many senior faculty for the junior
faculty to work with, to become active in research with.

Among other suspected reasons for leaving, salary was mentioned as a
primary motivating force in two cases, but the more typical comment

was: "They didn't offer him much more in the way of money, but he thought he would be more appreciated there."

Another frequently mentioned element in the voluntary departures of assistant professors was the spouse employment factor noted earlier: the spouse who could not find a good job, the new spouse who was somewhere else, the dual-career couple who found a better situation.

He has a professionally trained wife with a Master's degree in library science. The library here would not give her the time of day. She has a very good job with a publisher there.

They were sharing one and a third position here. She was on leave from a tenured position; they got some money and wanted her back badly. They wanted her husband, too, and they made a substantial offer with substantial research support. So they had a package where they could both be full salary and she a tenured associate professor.

Occasional aberrations in management appear in connection with assistant professor resignations, as in this description from a social sciences department:

We had a serious problem with the woman who was chairman while he was here. She was retired from another school and had a five-year contract here; it was her first administrative position and she was very authoritarian in her approach to administration. She became annoyed with him for not keeping office hours and had the telephone removed from his office!

As in 1958, the associate professor is the least likely (of the three academic ranks) to leave, and when he or she does resign, again as in the earlier study, it is often to go to a full professorship. The fourteen associate professors who resigned shared only five supposed reasons for leaving. In rank order, they were lack of promotion to full professor (five mentions); intellectual isolation (three); conflict with chairman or other senior person (two); and "personal" or entirely a matter of attraction to the new position (two each). Colleagues were generally sympathetic with the associate professor's feelings about lack of promotion, for example:

She was not happy when she left. She felt she had not been given the kind of consideration she deserved. She is an extremely important scholar in her field, and this is not necessarily measured by books. She has an international reputation. I think the mechanical approach by the [central tenure and promotion] committee is extremely shortsighted, stupid. There is no point in antagonizing people who are going to stay here as permanent members of the faculty even if they are not promoted.

Then there was the outlier:

He gave notice one week before the end of the semester. He made a killing in real estate and said to hell with it.

There were a variety of reasons proffered for the full professor resignations; most frequently mentioned were intellectual incompatibility with colleagues, lack of research support, hostility in the department, and personal reasons.

He felt that some of his colleagues in his own area here were not as intellectually stimulating as he would have liked.

He is an incredibly bright, outspoken, aggressive person and here those characteristics will get you nothing. They like WASPs with stiff upper lips who support the administration. He was not popular with his colleagues.

Probably the most important factor is that his prospective new wife is there and his old wife is here.

And there were some mentions—matching those noted earlier by newly appointed professors—of a "time to leave" feeling:

I had a long talk with him and he said to me, "I'm bored, I can see myself doing the same thing for the next twenty years that I did for the last twenty years; I want a change." He had been here since he got his Ph.D. He had reached the full professor rank. He had done everything he could do here and he wanted a different kind of experience.

"Pull" Factors

Those assistant professors who moved voluntarily within higher education were thought by colleagues to be attracted primarily by more compatible colleagues and a better place in which to pursue their research interests. These reasons are similar to those given by new appointees for selecting a job, as reported earlier. Also tied for first place, somewhat more important for this group of advanced assistant professors, was greater spouse employment opportunity, about evenly split between academic couples and couples in which one member was seeking a nonacademic job. Further down the list were tenure or tenure chances (not considered the most important reason in any case) and geographic location, the latter having some overlap with spouse employment. Incidentally, the comment closest to Caplow and McGee's "recorder" quote in a hiring situation occurs here, in reverse circumstances (and in the same institution):

I don't know what attracted him. There were people there he could work with on research. He is an excellent cello player and perhaps getting into Boston made a difference for him.

Associate professors and professors, in most cases, were thought to be attracted by more prestigious positions—full or distinguished professorships, or administrative responsibilities of a highly influential nature.

He went to a university in Germany that is well known in the field. He became a professor of the old school. To emigrate is a significant move to make in one's life. He spent a lot of time in Germany over the years and was extremely well known there. They offered him an opportunity to be a professor in the German style, teach when and whatever he wants and have assistants and so forth.

Seen in second place for associate professors were geographic location and spouse employment. Close to first place for professors were research support and research interests. Again, these reasons are similar to those reported earlier by new appointees. For example, compare the reported reason for this departure with a new appointee's account of space and research support in the previous chapter:

He was attracted to a chair. The salary was significantly higher, but it also carried an endowment for research—that was a factor that really attracted him. He has twice as much space plus an equivalent amount to be remodeled later.

Not to be overlooked is the academic gadfly:

He had accepted the position and then declined and then undeclined. He is not going to stay, though. He is moving on to Berkeley. He is the kind of person who is always on the market.

Six months after he came here he took a sabbatical leave there and we knew he was being courted. At the time he came he was on leave in Europe, then he was here for a semester, and then on leave there. He flew there from Europe to interview without bothering to stop here and tell us about it. He is very plugged in to information networks, always looking.

She has a wanderlust. Actually we did well to keep her for five years. She's a restless person. She only stayed there a year and has now moved on.

The actual content of the new academic job differed very little from the one left. Exceptions were movements into the European system and two moves to different disciplines, with one of those and one other within a discipline split between an academic department and an interdisciplinary research center. There were several mentions of a change in teaching—e.g., "Less teaching but more in his specialty"; "She is teaching a wider range"; "He teaches only graduate students."

Among assistant professors, of those who moved voluntarily, thirteen (32 percent of the total) were promoted to associate professor at the new position, and of those who were denied tenure, a comparable thirteen (30 percent of the total) were promoted. Among associate professors,

five (36 percent) were promoted to full professor, and thirteen (22 percent) of the full professors who left were promoted to an endowed chair, a chairmanship, the directorship of an important program, or the presidency of a college or university.

As indicated by data presented earlier, the use of personal contacts in obtaining a job increases with the experience of the faculty member. Only 8 percent of this group were thought to have responded to advertisements, most of those at the assistant professor level. The principal factor in the job search was personal contact for 83 percent of the associate and full professors, 63 percent of the assistant professors. Ads were the principal factor in the job search for less than one percent of those in the senior ranks, and only 10 percent of the assistant professors.

Efforts to Retain

Efforts were made by the department to retain the resigning assistant professors and associate professors in about a third of the cases—roughly equivalent to the percentages found by Caplow and McGee—for fourteen out of the forty-one assistant professors and five out of the fourteen associate professors. The efforts consisted predominantly of salary counteroffers and a leave arrangement for the first year at another school. The latter, judging from the total sample including new appointees, was a common device used to provide a tie to the department in the hope that the faculty member would decide to return.

He was offered a position there and asked if he could have a year's leave to make up his mind. We were pleased to give him the leave because we thought it was to our advantage to keep him, but he decided to stay there.

These leaves might run as long as three years for a senior person, and this sample included one two-year leave at the assistant professor level, although the usual period is one year.

Reasons for not attempting to keep the faculty member ranged from a feeling of helplessness in the face of an excellent offer to a feeling of good riddance:

He was a shoo-in for tenure here, but we knew we couldn't compete with Harvard.

We decided not to match the offer. No one argued his ability as a scholar, but he was a real bastard. He is very difficult, I mean really difficult, in the classroom. This is one of the few times when we have been willing to say that even though the scholarship is okay, we would just as soon get rid of the person. He is first rate in his field but he drives people nuts.

Much more effort was expended on the full professors; eighteen of the twenty-six were the object of intensive efforts at retention—but almost exclusively the efforts were reduced to money! Inasmuch as the primary

motivation to move at this level was probably not salary- based (according to the previously reported interview data and other research), one could expect the efforts to be, in the words of one chairman, "too little, too late." But perhaps rejection, however, (as suggested by Caplow and McGee) is easier for the members of the losing department to accept if they are able to reduce the matter to simple economics. In one instance, though, the salary offer may have been more meaningful (although ultimately unsuccessful) because of colleague sacrifice involved. This system was unique in the sample and may be unique in the country:

We have a very specific system that was implemented a few years ago when the financial pinch made itself felt acutely. If you want to keep somebody, if you want to match an offer, the dean will match anything that the department is willing to give up of its salary raises. We have to put our money where our mouth is. The faculty supported him.

(But was the faculty convinced that he would leave anyway?)

In the eight cases where no efforts were made, the reasons fit the same pattern as that of assistant and associate professors: There was no use ("it was a *fait accompli*") or there was hostility toward him in the department. Indeed, one resignation had resulted from the department's insistence that the dean remove him as chairman—"We all breathed an extraordinary sigh of relief."

DESTINATION

Where did these departing faculty members go? To diverse places. Again using department rankings, Table 21 indicates some differentiation by rank and reason for leaving. The drift was decidedly downward for assistant professors, in the kind of move illustrated in this observation: "Well, he's in a weaker department, but he is a big fish in a small pond." But the downward drift did not rule for those at the more senior level, where more than half of the associate and full professors who moved to ranked departments maintained or improved their prestige level.

To elaborate on these data shown in Table 21:

- The dismissed assistant professors who went to A and C departments returned to temporary jobs at their Ph.D. institutions; one assistant professor in the "other" group went to Cambridge; the others went to U.S. institutions in departments not ranked.
- In the "other" group of assistant professors who resigned, four went to foreign schools, one to a professional school, and one to an administrative position.
- Among the associate and full professors in the "other" category, two went to foreign schools, one from a ranked department moved to an unranked discipline, and four took administrative jobs, including two college presidencies.

Table 21:
Destination of Departing Faculty Members

Academic Rank	Ranking* of Dept.	Total	A	B	C	D	E	LHE	Other
			Number of Departures						
			Destination						
			Ranking* of Departments						
Asst Prof (dismissed)	A	-							
	B	8			1	1	2	1	3
	C	15					1	9	5
	D	12	1		1		3	3	4
	NR	8						4	4
Total		43	1	-	2	1	6	17	16
Asst Prof (resigned)	A	1					1		
	B	7	1			1		2	3
	C	14	1		1	3	4	1	4
	D	10	2			1	2	3	2
	NR	9						4	5
Total		41	4	-	1	5	7	10	14
Assoc Prof and Prof	A	3		1				2	
	B	1	1						
	C	17	1	3	1	2	3	2	5
	D	10	1			2	1	5	1
	NR	9						3	6
Total		40	3	4	1	4	4	12	12

*A = Departments ranked 1-5   E = Departments ranked below 40
B = Departments ranked 6-10   NR = Department in a discipline not ranked
C = Departments ranked 11-20   LHE = Left higher education
D = Departments ranked 21-40

The substantial lateral and upward movement suggests a relaxation of the doctoral prestige theory with the acquisition of proven capabilities, but it may also reflect the greater demand for full professors in the current market. The departing faculty members, however, obtained their new positions primarily through personal contacts with colleagues to whom their reputations were known—a continued reliance upon acquaintanceship.

They approached him. Ours is a relatively small field and those kinds of positions become well known when they become available. It was through personal contact. It is relatively easy to identify major possibilities.

He is well known and was personally recruited. They tried to get him four or five years ago.

A disturbing comparison here is that between the percentage of faculty members leaving higher education now and those leaving in the 1958 study (see Table 22), or as one respondent commented (echoing Cartter's 1976 prophecy):

In the future the "marketplace" issue is not going to mean movements from one university to another but rather movements in and out (mostly out) of academia.

Although most pronounced among the dismissed assistant professors and the associate professors (in fact, full professors show a decrease), the overall effect is one of perceptible increase in the number of those leaving higher education.

A breakdown of assistant professors leaving higher education is presented in Table 23, showing disciplinary division, type of termination, ranking of the department where the assistant professor earned his or her doctorate, ranking of the department where he or she was employed, and destination upon leaving. Of the nineteen cases in ranked disciplines, thirteen were trained in top-ten departments—nine in top-five departments; all moved down in the rankings, and then out. It is unwise to read too much into these small numbers, but there is an

Table 22:
Faculty Members Leaving Higher Education

Academic Rank	Percent Leaving Higher Eduction	
	1958 Study	1986 Study
Assistant Professors--dismissed	27.3	39.5
Assistant Professors--resigned	23.5	24.4
Associate Professors	28.6	35.7
Professors	33.3	26.9
All Ranks	27.0	31.5

Note: Total terminations excluding deaths and retirements numbered 102 in 1958 and 124 in 1986.

Table 23:
Assistant Professors Leaving Higher Education

Disciplinary Division	Type of Termination	Ranking of Ph.D. Dept.	Ranking of Employing Dept.	Destination
Humanities:	Resignation	*	*	Consulting/self-employment
	Resignation	*	*	Government
	Resignation	11	6	Law school
	Resignation	14	20	Business school
	Dismissal	*	*	(unknown)
	Dismissal	1	23	Family business
	Dismissal	5	9	Consulting/self-employment
	Dismissal	5	19	Government
	Dismissal	7	17	Consulting/self-employment
	Dismissal	10	11	Industry
Social Studies:	Resignation	*	*	Consulting/self-employment
	Resignation	*	*	Family business
	Resignation	2	8	(unknown)
	Resignation	3	50	Consulting/self-employment
	Resignation	5	42	Government
	Resignation	6	8	(unknown)
	Dismissal	*	*	Government
	Dismissal	4	12	Business school
	Dismissal	6	12	Government
	Dismissal	4	23	Seminary
	Dismissal	47	29	Consulting/self-employment
	Dismissal	48	3	Consulting/self-employment
Natural Sciences:	Dismissal	*	*	Industry
	Dismissal	*	*	Consulting/self-employment
	Dismissal	4	11	Industry
	Dismissal	12	18	Industry
	Dismissal	33	23	Industry

indication that opportunities outside higher education are competing for the best trained people.

In illustration of what may be a new way of thinking about the application of doctoral study, here is a quote from an assistant professor of economics in his terminal year:

We all know the game—if we can't accept it we should get out, choose a different profession. We undergo brainwashing in graduate school. We are attracted by the lure of formulating and solving problems. But there are also problems to solve in the private sector. I may leave higher education.

RETIREMENT AND DEATH

The circumstances of faculty termination have changed dramatically with respect to retirement and death, reflecting the longer life span of today's faculty member. Death accounted for 11 percent of terminations in the earlier study; in the current study the proportion is only 3 percent. The retirements projected for the latter part of this century are already being felt slightly—at 23 percent of terminations in this 1984 sample.

The thirty-eight retirements covered a wide spectrum, including the relatively new phenomenon of "early" retirement, that is, occurring prior to the traditional normal retirement age of 65. Patton (1977) had looked at early retirement, finding that women were more likely than men to retire before the age of 65, and associate professors were more likely than members of other ranks to do so. Neither finding was supported by this study, although the numbers are too small to be conclusive. Early retirements accounted for less than a third of the total (twelve out of the thirty-eight), but all of the early retirees were men and only two were associate professors. There were two "involuntary"—that is, institution-initiated—retirements in the early retirement sample, one resulting from a severe decline in scholarship and the other from a criminal conviction. Two other early retirements were caused by poor health. In the other eight cases, the faculty member retired early because of favorable financial arrangements and a desire to shed at least some academic responsibilities, but in several cases not all such responsibilities.

Patton also noted that many retiring faculty members intended to remain active professionally. Of the thirty-eight retirees in the current study, twenty-nine remained professionally active after retirement, and thirteen of those continued teaching, advising students, or conducting research involving students in the department where they had been full-time members. One emeritus professor reported on his recent activity:

I just edited a book . . . I'm very active at present with other faculty and students on opposition to apartheid . . . I've also written chapters for two books to be published this year. . . . My scientific work continues with NIH funding; I have

an active laboratory studying cells of the immune system. I didn't retire because I disliked my faculty role, I wanted some years to do things outside my discipline.

Others were described by colleagues:

He has been active in many departmental doctoral advancement to candidacy committees in spite of his formal retirement. He remains a very active consulting colleague. His last book was published in the last two years.

He has a separate research organization that he is maintaining, mostly federally funded. He continues to publish. He goes to international conferences.

He saw retirement as an opportunity to do more of his research. He is an emeritus professor and has an office here in the department. He has been working on a mammoth history of literature—monumental. He has published four volumes, is working on the fifth.

The combination of early retirement and continuing work in the department beyond formal retirement suggests that retirement projections may be less specific than might be thought. Another unknown quantity at present is the effect of the new law prohibiting mandatory retirement. Bowen and Schuster (1986) suggest that already-conceived personal plans for the anticipated retirement years will cause the change in the law to have a minimal effect on retirement projections, and that view is generally supported by this study. The seven-year delay in application of the law to tenured professors will also probably serve to maintain expected retirement rates in the near future.

The retirees' past contributions to the department were viewed in a generally positive way in most instances, with very little disagreement between the chairmen and peers responding. There was, though, recognition of unsatisfactory elements in the faculty member's academic position prior to retirement—these could frequently be characterized as "generational" in nature:

He became disappointed in the tendency for more and more of the teaching of writing to devolve onto graduate students. He thought the way they were trained to teach was a little bit lax. He had been in charge of the freshman writing program and was old fashioned about form and style.

He was unhappy about the turn that the whole academic environment was taking. He was a very conservative person, reactionary, patriarchal. He was historically minded rather than critically minded. He frowned on all this new-fangled stuff!

And there were a few comments like these:

He was not a little embarrassment to the department when it started really developing in the 1970s. He had good rapport with students in the survey

courses at the elementary level, but he was never appointed to the graduate faculty when that was necessary before our reorganization. He isolated himself from the department.

She was a very contested teacher, in some ways very bad. She was not good with undergraduates but was good at the upper level. She absolutely refused to be a team worker and was very difficult to get along with.

Overall, the reaction of the faculty members to their retirement was considered by their colleagues to be positive. An emeritus professor himself reported the pleasure of escaping the "boredom of faculty meetings," and a colleague described another retiree's attitude in this way:

She was looking forward to having free time without all of the demands of committee work and faculty meetings and student exams, and so forth.

For most of those who were no longer professionally active, the prognosis was still positive, as in this example:

He finished the revision of his book shortly before he retired and decided to pursue his hobbies, music, etc. He moved to Chapel Hill. We invited him for a lecture recently and he said no, he wasn't keeping up with the field.

There were a few reports of reluctance about retiring or of missing teaching, and this rather poignant remark about a distinguished former chairman:

She said that she would look forward to it [retirement], that there were many things she wanted to do and that she didn't want an office here in the department, but she seems to be wandering around here, a little lonely.

IMPACT OF DEPARTURE

People have become more important to the academic department since Caplow and McGee's day, more than one might expect in a buyer's market, but not as much as one might expect in other respects. Now, as then, when well educated, experienced professionals leave an organization, it would be expected that their loss would be felt. Caplow and McGee expressed surprise that this was not the case in their sample, and conjectured that departure was perceived as rejection and caused a reluctance on the part of department members to acknowledge the full effect of departure. They commented further that the careful scrutiny of candidates for a faculty position and the complicated process of search and appointment implied a uniqueness in the appointee that was belied by the lack of impact of a departure on the department. There was no effect in more than 60 percent of the cases in their sample.

The same conditions held to a large extent in the current study, although the total no-impact group has dropped to 51 percent. Where

Table 24:
Impact of Faculty Departure on Department

	Proportion	
Unit of Comparison	Some Effect	No Effect
Institution:		
Public	48%	52%
Private	46%	54%
Disciplinary Division:		
Humanities	52%	48%
Social Sciences	49%	51%
Natural Sciences	42%	58%
Department Ranking*:		
1 to 10	35%	65%
11 to 20	44%	56%
21 to 40	47%	53%
Below 40	50%	50%
Academic Rank:		
Assistant Professors	37%	63%
Associate Professors	67%	33%
Professors--resigned	60%	40%
Professors--retired	62%	38%

*Jones et al. (1982)

Caplow and McGee found 50 percent of full professor terminations to have no effect, this study saw that proportion drop to 36 percent. Their 44 percent for associate professors has decreased to 33 percent in the 1986 study. As indicated in Table 24, the departure of assistant professors and natural scientists seemed to have the least impact on the department, and the top-ranked departments suffered less effect from a termination than did lower-ranked departments (but those departments also had far fewer terminations). Note that there was not much difference between the impact of the departure of professors who resigned and those who retired—casting some doubt on a rejection theory.

There is consistency in the parallels between the reasons for a departure having an effect or not having an effect. According to respondents, departures of junior faculty members had no effect on the department because the assistant professors who left were not successful in research, never had many students, had not been there long enough to make a difference, were not in the mainstream of the department's interests, were in a large department where one person did not matter much, or had been replaced satisfactorily. Respondents commented that

the departures had an effect on the department because it was difficult to find people in their particular fields, they were exceptionally good teachers, their area was left uncovered, it was a loss to the department's research effort, it was a small department and the loss of one person was felt, or the department lost the position.

There were few clues in the interview responses as to the real reasons behind impact or lack of impact. For example, following are ambiguous comments about assistant professors who were denied tenure in natural science departments, the first concerning two departures from the same subfield that purportedly had no effect on the department and the second about a person whose departure did have an effect:

[No effect:] Well, I suppose number theory is slightly diluted, but that has to be balanced against other considerations. When they were being considered for tenure, the department decided to try to get a stronger researcher from outside. We in fact did that. But he has been hired away from us by Columbia. We also had a young guy, who was stronger than either of them, but he was hired away by Stanford. So indirectly, it was a change for the department but the positions are still open and we are looking at a number of other number theorists that we might hire.

[Effect:] I was very sorry that as an experiment it didn't work out because I thought it was a revolutionary appointment at the time. No other department would make that sort of appointment, and so I was very disappointed. We're trying again with a brand new appointment. We were the first to try it.

Comments about departures at the senior level were similar to those made about assistant professors, but with the additional complaint that the departed faculty member had not been active enough in the department, had not made strong contributions to the department; in a few cases, as had been noted by Caplow and McGee as well, the senior faculty member had "left" the department for an administrative post within the university some time before actually leaving.

He had effectively withdrawn from the department. He had been an associate dean for many years. He had become absorbed by administration and realized he wouldn't get promoted.

Associate professors and professors were missed for the same reasons as assistant professors but also because of national or international prominence—loss of prestige for the department—and sometimes because it meant the loss of a hard-to-replace chairman or program director. Or just a loss of experience:

Well, they leave at the top, and we hire at the bottom. That means that we lose someone who can teach at a 360 degree coverage and gain someone who can teach only at a 180 degree coverage.

Also noted about professors by professors was the loss of a personal friend. There were references of this kind by former colleagues about assistant professors as well; they were sometimes couched in political terms:

People like the chairman breathe much easier now. Others of us miss the kind of interaction and discussions we had with him. The students definitely lost. He and I were teaching in the same field the same semester, and we often worked with each other's students. He was a lot of fun. A very good friend.

It was negative for me of course because he was my friend. It does shift the balance of power in the department concerning the future of the department as far as the younger members are concerned.

Only 38 percent of the responses indicated that a retiring faculty member's departure had no effect on the department, and in that case usually because they had become inactive in research or had become peripheral or even antagonistic toward the department. An effect was felt for most of the reasons noted above, but in addition it was often said about a retiree that the loss was *personal*, his going marked the "end of an era."

He stood for something that's not that common now. Most of his energy went into actual teaching. He thought there were certain old fashioned things you ought to do in learning Milton—for example, memorizing chunks of it. E. B. White's ideal of style was very important to him, and he worked very hard to get undergraduates to appreciate style. He thought what we were being paid to do was to be a rhetorician in the old fashioned sense. Now we think we are scholars first.

We replaced him with a vastly different kind of person. He was a scholar of the old tradition and respected for what he did, but this department has been moving in a different direction.

Finally, the real impact of departures on a department may be a future assessment. A department is likely to slip severely in the ratings when departures have a domino effect, that is, when more than one faculty member leaves in sequence. In one instance in this sample, where two senior people in the department had left, a junior faculty member announced a job offer in these succinct terms: "If rats can leave the sinking ship, so can a mouse."

6

Change and the Ivory Tower

The university retains aspects of the monastery.

PROFESSOR OF GEOGRAPHY

University administration is applied social science.

PROFESSOR OF GOVERNMENT

One of the great inventions of 20th-century America, the private corporation, has begun to displace, as a formal structure and as a style of management, the older ecclesiastical and academic structures and styles in which universities grew up.

A. BARTLETT GIAMATTI, FORMER
PRESIDENT OF YALE UNIVERSITY

The interview data and descriptive statistics in the preceding chapters furnish a sense of the change, or absence of change, that has occurred in the academic marketplace over the past thirty years. We have seen in Chapters 3 through 5, concerned with recruiting and separation, that the processes of perpetuating the faculty show the least change; the external forces affecting the personnel system described in Chapter 2 show the most change. A comparison of these findings with those of Caplow and McGee is shown in Table 25.

Put another way, there is less change in the elements controlled by the academic department—application of disciplinary prestige, employment practices, separation practices—and more change caused by the environment external to the department. Change is usually brought about by external conditions and resisted by the organism being changed; it would be expected that the academic department would be an "agent of nonchange." Organization theorists Hannan and Freeman (1977) have identified limitations on the ability of organizations to change; internal considerations that "generate inertia" include investment in specialization. The academic department is a highly specialized unit and indeed, in this study, appears to generate inertia, or at least not to overcome it.

The specialization of the academic department provides the connec-

Table 25:
1986 Study Findings by Change from 1958 Findings

Study Category	Change from 1958	No Change from 1958
Prestige System		Dominates the research university.
Market/Policies	Generally, increased supply and decreased demand.	Market differentiation among and within disciplines.
	Nonacademic competition for Ph.D.'s.	Importance of noneconomic factors to participants.
	Acceptance of women and minorities in labor market.	
	Spouse employment as market issue.	
	Research emphasis intensified and clarified; greater integration of teaching into research culture.	
	Disciplinary and institutional orientations not mutually exclusive.	
	Management strategies: resource allocation, planning, innovation, improving competitive position.	
Search	Codified procedures, including open advertising.	Screening criteria: letters of recommendation, research, publications/writing samples.

	Closer attention to credentials, e.g., reading of publications.	Importance of sponsorship; weight of personal contacts (nominators, recommenders) in obtaining positions.
		Department responsibility for search.
Selection	Importance of campus interview.	Selection essentially a subjective process.
	More negotiation at senior level of employment terms and conditions.	Pool of top candidates not deep.
	Junior faculty members viewed as more important to department.	Departments hire first or second choice.
	More lateral and upward movement at senior level.	Departmental responsiblity for selection.
		Offers made with administrative approval.
		Accommodation of special situations in "negotiated" positions.
Separation	Proportions of death, retirement.	Proportions of dismissal, resignation.
	"Motives for migration" more personal-career oriented."	Split responsibility for tenure denial, but predominantly a departmental decision.
		Salary peripheral to mobility decision.

tions to prestige, which originates in an academic discipline. Only geobarbanalysts can legitimately evaluate other geobarbanalysts, wherever they may be found. It is the traditional dependence of the Department of Geobarbanalysis on reputation ascribed by others that perpetuates the prestige system.

THE PRESTIGE PRINCIPLE

Prestige remains the oxygen of higher education—it permeates the atmosphere of the research university. Caplow and McGee viewed prestige as the virtual context of faculty mobility; prestige still plays a primary organizational role, sometimes more subtle, sometimes redefined, but always prominent in the thinking of academicians. The desire for prestige may be seen as a yearning toward increased status, or relative position, in a society that rank-orders everything from top forty records to the popularity of various members of the British royal family. The need to identify or seek status appears to be part of the human condition. It has been argued that a "relative standing" theory may supersede traditional market theory in many instances (Frank 1985); there seems to be some basis for applying a relative standing, or status, theory to universities. The prestige factor in a research university substitutes for the earnings ratio in a profit-making organization.

The use of prestige as a measure of success makes some nervous. Researchers frequently preface their comments about prestige, or ranking, or status, with admonitions against equating prestige with quality, but quality (not to be confused with "effectiveness," which nobody really has captured either) eludes adequate definition. Before explaining the methodology used in their assessment of research-doctorate programs, Jones and others (1982, p.13) quoted from Robert M. Pirsig's *Zen and the Art of Motorcycle Maintenance*:

Quality . . . you know what it is, yet you don't know what it is. But that's self-contradictory. But some things are better than others, that is, they have more quality. But when you try to say what quality is, apart from the things that have it, it all goes poof! There's nothing to talk about. But if you can't say what Quality is, how do you know what it is, or how do you know that it even exists? If no one knows what it is, then for all practical purposes it doesn't exist at all. But for all practical purposes it really does exist. What else are grades based on? Why else would people pay fortunes for some things and throw others in the trash pile? Obviously some things are better than others . . . but what's the "betterness"? . . . So round and round you go, spinning mental wheels and nowhere finding anyplace to get traction. What the hell is Quality? What is it?

Undaunted, Jones and his colleagues surveyed thousands of faculty members to obtain disciplinary assessments of the quality of graduate

programs in the United States. The results appeared to show, in the high correlations between reputational survey and more concrete measures such as research expenditures and publications, that prestige was, if not equated with quality, at least anchored in the realm of quality.

With that caveat, we can state the prestige principle: The quality of a research university is centered in the prestige of its academic departments, and the prestige of the academic department depends upon the individual reputations, drawn from the discipline at large, of its faculty members.

Given the unchanging nature of prestige in the academic setting, and the inertia generated by the academic department, it is not surprising to find the ways and means of acquiring and shedding faculty members, which are controlled by the academic department, displaying little change.

STAFFING PATTERNS

A thread of prestige-consciousness is woven throughout the recruitment process. The "top twenty places" are contacted in order to ensure that the best people apply; letters of recommendation from writers "with some reputation" are valued. A select group of "senior people" here and in other countries are contacted for nominations. Affirmative action has not made the dent that had been feared by some: The opportunities for blacks are present "if they go to the right schools." The search for faculty is quite dependent upon that somewhat intangible notion of status; even where a chairman avers that some of the "prestige thing is prejudice," his department had hired a Harvard Ph.D.

So, in spite of the much broader communication of information about today's faculty openings, faculty hiring is still the closed, or preferential, system that Caplow and McGee described. Beyond a certain threshold of ability, in which doctoral prestige plays a part, a candidate is judged initially on his or her professional reputation as ascribed by others in the discipline.

The initial advertising of a position does have the result of much larger applicant pools for junior positions than were present in the Caplow and McGee study (although there is little change in the applicant pools for senior positions). The increase in total numbers, however, has not changed the number of finalists for the position; the pool of acceptable (i.e., best) applicants is not deep. Occasionally at the junior level and always at the senior level, outstanding candidates are specifically identified and aggressively recruited.

As for selection procedures, the most prominent change from the Caplow and McGee study is the critical importance of the campus interview at the junior level and its occurrence in modified versions (but

taking a subordinate position to professional reputation) at the senior level as well. We might view the emergence of firsthand evaluation of candidates by department members as a universalistic practice contributing to a more open system, as opposed to ascription, were it not for the fact that no one reaches the interview stage without surviving the initial screening and, as has been noted, the pool of finalists is never deep.

An ascriptive recruiting system makes sense in choosing professionals, who function autonomously and whose potential performance cannot be assessed with a great degree of certainty. Dornstein (1977) noted a parallel in executive recruitment. Like faculty members, her executives were highly autonomous and it was difficult to assess their quality. The executive recruitment process, by depending upon sponsorship, allowed a function of preselection, lessening the danger that the person would not support the values of the corporation—in the language of this study, "fit in."

An example even more relevant than Dornstein's executives is that of the similarity between the recruitment of faculty professionals and that of research professionals outside academia in Dill's (1985) research. In a study of research and development managers, he differentiated between "coarse sifting" (open recruiting procedures) and "fine sifting" (preferential recruiting procedures). Coarse sifting employs, for example, general advertisements in newspapers or professional publications. Fine sifting may include advertisements, but features personal contacts to identify candidates, particularly aggressive individualized pursuit of talented individuals, and the importance of the job interview. Fine sifting procedures clearly apply to faculty recruitment, paralleling those procedures used to recruit researchers in the research and development organizations. Dill found that the process ensured a group of finalists "as homogeneous as possible on the critical dimension of scientific skill and knowledge" (p. 230). The respondents in this study made comparable statements about their finalists. In both settings, fine sifting reduced uncertainty about the professional competence of the candidates.

Where change has occurred in the faculty staffing process, the fine-sifting characteristics have not been diluted. There is more attention given to the individual during recruiting—e.g., in the reading of publications, the campus interview. There is also an increasing appreciation for the potential contribution of the new junior faculty member to the academic department. Neither the attention nor the appreciation, however, has an impact on the ascriptive nature of the initial screening of candidates or on the select pool of finalists from which the new faculty member is chosen.

A separate question is how well the preferential hiring system works in predicting "good fit," that is, in minimizing faculty turnover.

FACULTY TURNOVER

A critical concern of the department-building faculty, especially as the market tightens in the 1990s, should be reasons for voluntary resignation. Perhaps the most important finding here is the change from Caplow and McGee's motives for migration of prestige, security, and authority to a much more personal career framework—"he thought he would be more appreciated there." This point is often missed by faculty and administrators faced with a resignation. For example, although salary was rarely a primary motivator toward movement at any rank in this study, or in previous studies, it is still relied upon heavily in attempts to retain the departing faculty member. (These data, of course, do not include any faculty members who may have been enticed to stay by negotiated salary increases; but it is possible in such cases that salary merely outweighed the upheaval of moving at that particular time, without addressing the real causes of discontent. There is, too, the dubious practice of getting an offer to get a raise, which implies poor organizational policies and relationships.)

Retention, like staffing, is primarily the responsibility of the department. The new assistant professor is socialized in the department, not the larger university, and his or her success depends upon that socialization. The faculty member of any rank who leaves the organization voluntarily usually does so as a result of departmental, not institutional, relationships affecting his or her career. Strong identification of the professional with the "local clan" was suggested by Wilkins and Ouchi (1983); the interview data of this study are clear in showing the departmental identification of the faculty member. In fact, variance in the study occurred primarily at the departmental level—indicating the strong role of the academic department in the faculty personnel system and hence in faculty careers. The professional performance of the individual faculty member has a strong link to the department. Kanter (1983) observed that the actions of the individual in an organization often stem from the organizational context rather than factors internal to the individual. We could expect the organizational context—for example, an environment supporting an individual's research interests—to be particularly important in the realm of intellectual work in which a faculty member is involved.

The involuntarily terminated faculty member who achieves success at another university may call the judgment of the dismissing faculty into question, but is not a loss to the academic profession. Aggravating the consequences of faculty turnover for higher education is the larger proportion of departing faculty members who are leaving higher education completely—a larger proportion of faculty members than that in the 1958 sample, but also a larger proportion of faculty members than per-

sons leaving comparable professions. An analysis of census data by Otto and others (1980) shows the comparison between college teachers and professions that are similar across the dimensions of general educational development, specific vocational preparation, and overall complexity of work (see Figure 2): The proportion of college teachers leaving their profession, at 20 percent, is considerably higher than the 5, 7, and 10 percent shown for the comparable professions. (The rate for college teachers in the Otto study, 20 percent, is slightly higher than the projected rate of 17 percent for a comparable period in this study of research universities.)

Adding professions (in Group II of Figure 2) where one of the dimensions is scored lower than college teachers still shows disparity.

At first glance, it might be thought that salary level could be an explanatory variable in the higher incidence of departure for college teachers, and personal income may in fact contribute to the stability of professions such as physician, dentist, and lawyer. In this sample, however, only two people voluntarily leaving higher education were perceived to be motivated primarily by higher earnings. The defection from higher education appears to be caused by one or more of several factors, such as: fewer academic jobs to which the faculty member might move, challenging nonacademic opportunities, academic strife that creates feelings of disillusionment, a general loosening of commitment to academics. Any of these is a cause for concern within the academic profession.

Faculty mobility occurs, however, for knowable reasons, some of which could be influenced by organizational behavior. Schein (1975, 1978) has developed the concept of "career anchors" in a study of MIT's Sloan School of Management alumni. He contended that work careers reflect both individual and organizational definitions of worthwhile activity, and there is a need for organizations to help their members recognize those facets of their careers that furnish satisfaction—and become active elements in retention. The exploration of academic career anchors might shed significant light on faculty turnover and lead to a reduction of disaffection in academic organizations. (Some work has been done in this direction by James Bess in his 1982 book.)

The absence of an up-to-date human resource management context is also indicated by the fact that the departure of a faculty member still has surprisingly little effect on the department. This is a particularly puzzling contradiction to the increased expectations of the influence of the new faculty member that were expressed by respondents in this study. Although generally not reflected in recruiting, by the time termination occurs there has been a shift in personnel philosophy that best matches the "replaceable parts" tenet of scientific management. As Kanter (1983) pointed out, in the early 1900s individuals constituted sources of error

Figure 2
Departure from Profession (Age Cohort 33–37)

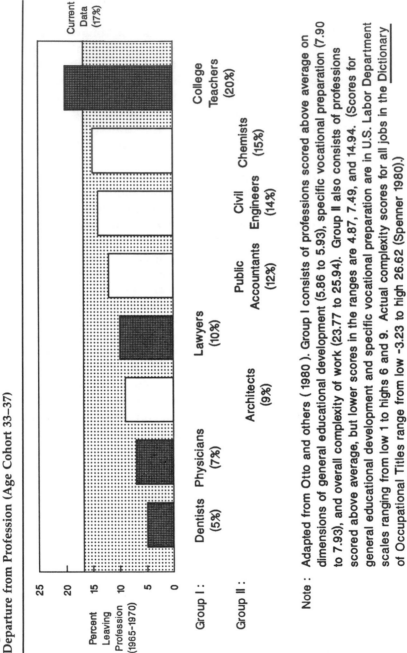

25
20
Percent 15
Leaving
Profession 10
(1965-1970)
5
0

Group I :   Dentists   Physicians   Lawyers   College
            (5%)   (7%)   (10%)   Teachers
                                                                                        (20%)

Group II :   Architects   Public   Civil   Chemists
                        (9%)   Accountants   Engineers (15%)
                                                      (12%)   (14%)

                                                                               Current
                                                                               Data
                                                                               (17%)

Note : Adapted from Otto and others (1980). Group I consists of professions scored above average on
        dimensions of general educational development (5.86 to 5.93), specific vocational preparation (7.90
        to 7.93), and overall complexity of work (23.77 to 25.94). Group II also consists of professions
        scored above average, but lower scores in the ranges are 4.87, 7.49, and 14.94. (Scores for
        general educational development and specific vocational preparation are in U.S. Labor Department
        scales ranging from low 1 to highs 6 and 9. Actual complexity scores for all jobs in the Dictionary
        of Occupational Titles range from low -3.23 to high 26.62 (Spenner 1980).)

rather than assets; this is the interpretation that is often seen in departmental attitudes toward termination.

Not to be discounted is the "peculiar institution" of graduate training, where the employer in its dual role also furnishes the labor supply. It is too easy for the faculties that prepare junior faculty to slip into a continuing mode of "grading" the former student. The new assistant professor is viewed not so much as a fellow professional as an object of continuing training who will not really prove himself or herself for seven or eight years—and then not on the basis of having performed a job well but on the basis of comparison with a somewhat hypothetical group of contemporary scholars somewhere. It may be that the mentality of "hiring better than we have" produces a "grass is always greener" posture that fails to recognize value in the individuals on hand.

It is in this willingness to discard professionals that we see the insidious facet of the prestige principle. Paul Dressel has said that the quality of a department is drawn from a prestigious minority of its members. Yet, every junior faculty member being appraised for tenure by his or her older colleagues of varying competence is expected to display star quality—and to be judged, not by co-workers who are members of the local clan, but by outsiders (who may have various axes to grind). In a world where the difference in attraction between faculty and nonfaculty employment for a Ph.D. is not so great as it once was, the disparity of treatment may prove to be a significant factor in career choices.

The grass-is-greener philosophy has an effect on senior faculty as well. Playing the ratings game motivates some departments to use senior level recruiting as a primary vehicle for acquiring a better score. In reality, it appears difficult to move into the top ten from a position below that group, and the interview data suggest that research universities may be endangering the future stability of their professional staffs by aggressive pursuit of an unrealistic rating goal through "restaffing." As the market changes and mobility opportunities increase, the departments that have been most ruthless in displacing their senior scholars may be faced with excessive turnover at a time when those departments can least afford it.

Thus, we see that the faculty personnel process is tied to "ecclesiastical and academic" origins through a dominant prestige system that results in largely unaltered staffing patterns and an acceptance of turnover. On the other hand, there is evidence in this study of the structures and styles of the "private corporation" through a new awareness of market conditions and management strategies.

Consequently, the "agent of change" in the faculty personnel system is found in those relationships between the organization and the social environment that now affect faculty mobility. In this study, the influences came predominantly from the current state of the academic labor

market and the policy responses made within the academic market-place.

MARKET EFFECTS

The most obvious change in the market is in demand and supply: there was great demand for faculty members and short supply of Ph.D.'s in the late 1950s; there is less demand and a larger supply in the 1980s. This change has effected a codification of recruitment procedures, a routinization of process across disciplines and research universities.

What has not changed about the market structure is the stratification of the academic labor market, preventing the interchangeability of employers and employees. In this sample the stratification is among disciplines and subfields with, for example, "500 ads" for computer scientists and "ten academic positions" in immunology, opportunities in the anthropology of health in developing countries but few in Arabic studies.

Stratification is also evidenced in the trickle-down effect, which is confirmed by the numerous appointments of Ph.D.'s from prestigious programs to lower-ranked departments. But in spite of fears of competition in the market from persons so placed, this sample of ninety-six assistant professor appointments included only one advanced assistant professor moving up from initial underplacement. If one ninety-sixth is typical, the movement up from trickling down has not substantially increased the complexity of the market in the research university since 1958.

The complexity has been affected, however, by other characteristics of the participants in the academic market. They are more diverse demographically, they are highly research-oriented and, some think, they are of better quality, and most agree not worse. They have more employment opportunities outside academia, and according to Bowen and Schuster (1986) those opportunities are likely to increase. Indeed, a more important market condition of the future may be the competition for Ph.D.'s from outside academia, as suggested by aspects of the differentiation of the academic labor market and by the incidence of faculty members leaving higher education. This study tells us that industrial jobs have changed the market "very dramatically"—even offering postdoctoral study. Nonacademic employment for Ph.D.'s has become "socially acceptable." There are "problems to solve in the private sector" that may draw Ph.D.'s away from higher education.

Along with the loosening of the academic world's hold over the Ph.D., we have seen the importance of quality of life issues, including the aspirations of dual-career couples. They bring to the academy from the social environment a new problem, spouse employment, that is apparently having a profound effect on faculty mobility.

Looking outward, the changed external environment of higher education has contributed heavily to another change in academe: A thriving market for research has been created. Apart from the needs of business and industry, a major component in itself, the complexity of national and international problems gives new currency to the academic researcher's expertise; as a practical illustration, not a week goes by on National Public Radio's morning news program without one or more taped interview excerpts with a faculty member of one of the nation's colleges or universities. We need the knowledge, often forged out of disagreement, that emanates from the research and scholarship nurtured in our universities.

RESEARCH EMPHASIS

The university's primary mission is research, but teaching is important as well. Prestige radiates from research: The geobarbanalyst at Chicago who rates the geobarbanalyst at Stanford does so on the basis of the latter's research papers, with which the former is familiar, not on teaching ability, about which he or she knows nothing. On the other hand, the geobarbanalyst at Chicago who rates his or her own Ph.D. is likely to refer to teaching ability in a letter of recommendation. Caplow and McGee perceived a split in the organizational culture between research and teaching interests—that faculty members were hired to teach but evaluated on their research productivity. On the surface it would appear that the conflict is a continuing condition; however, this study found no disagreement in the recruitment process on task and evaluation. New assistant professors had been trained to do research in graduate school, they liked research, and they chose jobs on the basis of research opportunities. Likewise, faculties perpetuating themselves chose as new assistant professors those persons who were doing "interesting, exciting work"—who would add to the prestige of the department by being known for that work. But teaching was also a criterion of selection: "We take teaching very seriously." Faculty members referred to themselves as "teachers," and linked their research interests to their teaching.

This is a murky area for the research university. The major mission of the institution is indeed research, but the place is full of students. How to mesh the two? Drawing from personal conversations with 266 faculty members of research universities, I conclude that the meshing has been done. I say this notwithstanding expert, but possibly not fully informed, opinions to the contrary. There is a concern for students and a concern for teaching present among the faculty members of research universities that is congruent with their research interests and the creation of new knowledge. Certainly, research *is* first, both chronologically and as a research university priority. A problem arises when teaching becomes

an isolated activity, not connected with research, either in reality or in the minds of critics of research universities.

In pondering the widespread, and I think undeserved, criticism of universities in their teaching role, it occurs to me that at least some of the criticism may stem from a basic misinterpretation of higher education in the university. The undergraduate years in a university are not an extension of K-12; this is a new venture for the entering freshman, a choice, the step beyond compulsory public education. It is entirely appropriate to place a good deal of the responsibility for education on the student at this point. The research university should draw the undergraduate who wants to participate more fully in his or her own education, and who has some understanding of the broader responsibilities—and opportunities—of the research university. And a little understood but significant advantage of the research university is the cadre of teaching assistants available from its graduate programs. Graduate assistants are frequently dedicated teachers who are enthusiastic about their subject matter and who have a strong interest in undergraduate students, enhancing the undergraduate experience. Given the characteristics of the research university, many of them advantageous to intellectual climate, the quality of undergraduate education at a university may be *different* but it is not inferior; the balance of teaching and research may not suit everyone but in the American system of stratified higher education it need not suit everyone.

The balance of teaching and research in the research university is clarified further by the change from Caplow and McGee's notion of disciplinary or institutional orientation ("cosmopolitan" or "local"). This study found the status of cosmopolitan important to mobility (one had to be known in the discipline in order to move); but the study also identified a career cycle that appeared to match a life cycle, with becoming known in the discipline a "young" activity and closer identification with both institution and discipline as "aging" takes place.

The fusing of the local and cosmopolitan orientations of professionals has also been studied in nonacademic organizations, notably by Goldberg (1976), who conducted a study of graduates of an Israeli engineering school. He found that an orientation that combined *both* cosmopolitan and local reference groups was more compatible with values and behaviors associated with professionalism than was a solely cosmopolitan reference group. Further, he found that contradictions could be traced to situational influences, such as career stage, occupational role primacy, and quality of the work environment. Quality of the work environment for a faculty member in a research university undoubtedly relies heavily upon research opportunities and support.

Included in the research environment are opportunities for collaboration. Caplow and McGee studied collaboration to ascertain its effect on

mobility and found none; the same is true in this study. In relation to research emphasis, however, another question may be the effect collaboration has on the individual faculty career: In this study collaboration was taking place between departed faculty members and members of the department, had taken place between members of the department and new appointees before they had become members of the department, and was taking place between new appointees in the department and members of other departments in the institution. Collaboration, therefore, may be a byproduct of individual research interests that cross organizational boundaries. In fact, the research emphasis has led to various kinds of research centers and institutes, and to interdisciplinary and multidisciplinary research in other forums. As the knowledge base has exploded, the narrowing of specialization appears to have encouraged new forms of collaboration toward new ways of knowing—"A lot of people feel their discipline is getting obsolete."

ORGANIZATIONAL CONCERNS

Caplow and McGee included in *The Academic Marketplace* a discussion of organizational perceptions and concerns based upon their research. These ranged from a typology of chairmen to stresses within the organization and problems of organizational units and members. Their observations, informed by their experience, led to the eleven recommendations included in their book; a review of those recommendations offers another perspective on change.

Recommendations 1 and 2

These two recommendations suggested a tenure rank of lecturer and strengthening seniority, both designed to provide institutional rather than disciplinary rewards, as a means of reducing turnover. Neither recommendation has been implemented overtly in research universities.

With a research culture so firmly entrenched in the research university, it seems unlikely that the first recommendation is tenable, or that the second is relevant. "Research is *first*," as agreed upon by the academic departments and the Ph.D.'s seeking jobs; the tenure-track lecturer rank would probably not be attractive to faculty members, even if it were adopted. As for the strengthening of seniority, identification with the institution does increase with seniority, implying some kind of reward, if less tangible.

Recommendations 3, 4, and 6

These are recommendations dealing with the terms and conditions of employment—base salaries, standard teaching loads, fringe benefits—

and also aimed at reducing turnover. Standard teaching loads, according to the respondents in this study, have been substantially implemented, with variations within an institution based on type of course.

Standard base salaries may have been adopted in all of the universities in this study—and there is anecdotal evidence supporting such an assumption—but salaries are public knowledge only in the public universities. Whether this secretive behavior in private universities is either necessary or desirable is certainly a debatable point that, although not a major concern of the respondents in this study, did appear as a contributing factor in expressions of dissatisfaction. Caplow and McGee commented as follows: "An auxiliary function of salary secrecy is to cloak inequitable treatment of individuals. We submit that a policy of strict equity may be the best reliance of the rational administrator in the long term" (*Marketplace*, pp. 241–242). Their statement needs no further comment.

Then we have fringe benefits. Generally, this recommendation has been implemented in the research university, with one notable exception, "reserved parking on campus" (*Marketplace*, p. 246). We are reminded of Clark Kerr's (1963) description of the modern university as a "series of individual faculty entrepreneurs held together by a common grievance over parking" (p. 20).

Recommendation 5

As noted earlier, it is irrelevant in its original sense of delaying tenure, but has been implemented essentially in the seven- to eight-year probationary period for an assistant professor, and the use of the untenured associate professor rank and non-tenure- track appointments. I would argue that, in the tradition of problem propagation (solutions create new problems), implementation of this recommendation has led to new problems for the faculty personnel system in the 1990s, in the growth of class distinctions within the faculty.

Recommendations 7 and 10

These recommendations called for a reduction of the "personal and arbitrary control" over faculty members by administrative officers and for orderly promotion procedures. Neither remains a matter of contention. There were no incidents reported of arbitrary behavior of individual administrators toward individual faculty members in any of the 306 interviews, although faculty colleagues themselves were sometimes guilty parties! (An exception might be the chairman who removed a faculty member's telephone, but she herself was "removed" by the dean shortly after that incident.)

Promotion procedures, albeit not always accepted without criticism,

were represented anecdotally as having structure similar to appointment procedures, a point confirmed in the written procedural material
collected from each institution. I would say that the argument here has
shifted, in a minority of instances, to focus on the decisions of an "un-
knowable" central faculty committee whose collective judgment is not in
agreement with that of a departmental faculty. This was not, however, a
widespread concern in the study sample.

Recommendations 8 and 9

These called for improved recruitment procedures and have been
implemented.

Recommendation 11

This recommendation asked that faculty positions be established on
the basis of need—a fact of life in the contemporary research university.

The substantial implementation of Caplow and McGee's recommendations illustrates a number of ways in which, using Giamatti's phras-
ing, universities have grown up in the past several years. There appears
to be less conflict between academic departments and central academic
administrators as department chairmen have assumed a larger leadership role in the organization. Faculty recruiting is characterized by orderly procedure and greater access. There is agreement between academic departments and job-seekers as to career and performance
expectations. Thus, although there may be a tendency toward increased
bureaucracy and organizational norms, there seems to be an accom-
panying tendency toward greater cohesiveness and less conflict in the
organization than was observed by Caplow and McGee.

A more appropriate conclusion to the current study than those concerns of Caplow and McGee, then, is consideration of the "management
revolution" in the research university. As we saw in Chapter 2, management strategies are important in the new academic marketplace. Strategic thinking has led to a firmer policy of centralized resource allocation,
whereby deans and provosts set academic goals and authorize recruitment accordingly. Cyert (1982) called this behavior developing a "comparative advantage"—finding the strengths of the organization on
which excellence can be based and building from those strengths.
Caplow and McGee pointed out (foreseeing a sense of "strategic planning" long before the terminology was invented) that this judgment was
the "proper business of provosts and deans" (*Marketplace*, p. 254). This
study, however, adds the dimension of the academic department, expanding the responsibility to include chairmen. Department chairmen

were directly involved not only in strategies focusing on faculty recruitment and development, but in departmental planning, serving as a resource for the administration in the latter role.

The strategic planning that the research university has borrowed from the private corporation, though, may not be sufficient. The long-term effectiveness of the strategic planning, marketing, and management control that have been embraced by universities, is in fact being seriously questioned within the best firms of the business community. In many leading corporations, there is greater attention to human resources management emerging, particularly within a context of organizational culture. To take the next step toward better utilization of resources, higher education is urged toward "management of academic culture: the nurturing of the expressive life of academic institutions and the strengthening of social integration" (Dill 1982, p. 319).

In the research university we have a strong beginning in the research culture that has developed over the years. An important item on the agenda should be greater integration of human resource management into the organizational culture. To facilitate our thinking on that subject, consider the results of a top-level meeting described by Walton and Lawrence (1985). In May 1984, twelve senior executives from major U. S. corporations met at Harvard with twenty-three members of the business school faculty in a colloquium designed to consider the trends and prospects for human resource management in American industry. Participants concluded that a major, nonreversible change toward what they called "mutuality" was under way*. The executive participants saw three forces driving change in human resource management: "changing values, intensified competition, and advanced information technology" (p. 353). They spoke of seeking a better way of working with people, reducing waste and conflict, in order to make the organization more effective—surely a reasonable goal for the academic organization as well.

Academia could learn from their results. Translated easily from nonacademic organizations into the terms of the data in this study, the three forces affecting academic human resource management are: (1) changing values that cause phenomena such as a mobility motivator of quality of life and a mobility issue of spouse employment; (2) intensified competition among research universities and between academic and nonacademic opportunities for Ph.D.'s; and (3) advanced information technology that locates the faculty member in a research community established through a global communication network of research and

---

*The importance of improved human resource utilization to the contemporary firm is also emphasized by writers such as Drucker (1981), Mitroff (1983), Reich (1983), Thurow (1985).

scholarship. These forces are pushing higher education toward a more effective management of human resources.

In order to survive, the university has attempted to move beyond the inept financial management of the past to the strategic management of the present. Now, the quality needs of the research university are pulling the institution away from outdated philosophies of managing people toward a more coherent organizational culture.

THOUGHTS FOR THE FUTURE

The organizational dilemma of the faculty personnel system in the research university derives largely from the contradiction inherent in the prestige principle: Prestige based on research is both a disruption to organizational culture and the basis for that culture. The disruption to the organizational culture occurs when persons who are not members of the organization make personnel judgments for the organization, and when individual faculty members achieve independence from the organization through disciplinary recognition. On the other hand, the research basis of the organizational culture depends upon the reputation of individual departments, and upon the reputations of members of the department, who are in turn dependent upon the judgments of persons who are not members of the organization. Thus, beyond the tensions and conflicts normally found among people in organizations, the university must grapple with the tension between the external professional influences of the guild (much stronger and more intrusive than any labor union) and the internal flexibility necessary to the health of a complex organization.

We have seen prestige adding value to the individual and strengthening the department in the fine-sifting of the recruiting process (although the process itself could be improved in some respects, such as follow-up communication with candidates), but we have seen its negative effects in retention—"people in the academic world don't make academic assessments." We have seen the alienated faculty member leave an oligarchical department—"conflict with a senior person." We have seen the importance of personal research interests in the department—"The interdisciplinary opportunities are very important to me." These three points exemplify external influences of the prestige system that reach down in the academic organization to the level of the production unit, the academic department.

What can be suggested by this study that would be of value in managing the conflict and building the organizational culture, particularly by improving integration at the boundaries of organizational units? I say "suggested" because the purpose of this book is not prescriptive. As the departmental variance in the study indicates, there is no best way, nor a one-two-three sequence of universal recommendations to be drawn

from these data. Nevertheless, implications of desirable change can be drawn from the study to assist in culture-building:

1. *Change in the perception and evaluation of junior faculty as members of the organization, including consistency in policy and practice across hiring and retention processes.*

In treatment of the junior faculty member in the hiring and retention processes, tension is caused by inconsistency of perception. At the recruitment stage, the prestige principle is positive, permitting the careful selection and evaluation of the individual; he or she is viewed as a valuable resource by the department. There is, however, a high failure rate reflected in dismissals, and there is a low incidence of impact on the department at departure; under the prestige principle, the assistant professor may be converted into disposable goods, a replaceable part. The staffing needs of the future may well call for a more flexible personnel approach to the junior professional.

A more flexible approach may, in turn, call into question continuance of the tenure system as it is now constituted. The pressure involved in making the tenure decision no doubt results in many poor decisions. We saw, for example, that retirement projections were higher for lower-ranked departments, implying that a lesser quality accompanies tenuring-in (and the tenure denial rate has not changed from that of thirty years ago). We also saw a number of presumably well trained professionals being driven out of higher education, predominantly from lower-ranked departments where external judgments would more likely supersede internal opinions. Although the tenure problem is not a simple one, it is already being "solved" in less obvious ways. For example, in a case that was not atypical, in one of the research universities in the study sample 55 percent of the fifty-eight appointments made were not tenure-track appointments. This use of non-tenure-track appointments has created the concept of a two-class faculty that contributes nothing to the health of the organization. Even when the appointment is renewable, as most are, and even where an individual has served for many years, as some have, the faculty member in such an appointment is viewed differently from the "regular rank" faculty.

There are, of course, numerous defenses of tenure in the literature (all written by tenured professors), but it would appear that relief from the tenure system could greatly enhance the organizational culture and improve human resource management. Many of the respondents in this study were troubled by the tenure system; a system of employment contracts that would include an academic freedom clause, as some suggested, might be preferable to the current situation.

2. *Change in the management orientation of the academic work group, accentuating the participative and deemphasizing the political.*

In retention of the senior faculty member, the prestige principle works to the faculty member's advantage. We have seen in the movement of

experienced people in this study, whether as appointments or departures, that prestige shifts from site to individual over time, that is, experienced faculty members carry their prestige with them. The human resource problem here is that mobility motivators are not sufficiently recognized nor understood, leaving the organization at the mercy of the application of the prestige principle by a recruiting department elsewhere.

It would seem important to try to determine the reasons for senior faculty mobility and to create an environment in which the faculty member would want to remain. There are, of course, some conditions that could not be changed—for example, the "old wife here, new wife there" or "time to leave" situations. Frequently, however, the data show that there is dissension or domination within a department that forces out a productive faculty member.

This brings us to the shortcomings of collegiality. Although departmental decisions are described as collegial and "participatory"—that is, everyone takes part—the truly participative management that builds a strong organization frequently is not present in an academic department. Democracy in the academy is not quite the same thing. Where department faculties vote, a political process is present; factions are likely to hold sway, and the successful factions will be led by those faculty members with the most prestige. Again, the extraorganizational influence is felt in organizational decisions. The consensus necessary for genuine participative management is rare; it was present in only a few departments in this study sample. The more common example, the tradition of secret ballot voting in departmental personnel matters, epitomizes a grave problem in university human resource management: the secretiveness, often euphemized as confidentiality, that pervades much of the faculty personnel process. The qualities of communication, openness, and trust that are necessary in building or reinforcing the organizational culture may be missing from the departmental scene.

It would appear that knowledge and practice of participative management techniques, with more emphasis on group cohesiveness, could be of significant benefit to the academic culture. There is some sensitivity developing at the departmental level about positive organizational behavior, as in the remarks by the chairman who understood the desirability of bringing his department to consensus in hiring decisions. Movement toward greater openness and trust should be encouraged.

3. *Change in the organizational structure of the university toward greater flexibility in accommodating new knowledge and research needs.*

There is general agreement that the department is the basic unit of the university, the part of the organization where the members of the organization responsible for the production function of the university—teaching and research—are housed. This is the front line, the entity from which the reputation of the university emanates.

Caplow and McGee stated that the academic department might be the most interesting part of the university to researchers because of the involvement and commitment of department members. Further, they believed that the "process by which a department replaces its members and maintains its immortality is as nearly central to an understanding of academic institutions as anything can be" (*Marketplace*, p. 28). We have seen that this process is still central to the labor-intensive university organization and still controlled by the academic department.

We have also seen the research interests of individuals changing the university through collaboration of various kinds, often resulting in multidisciplinary or interdisciplinary research. It has become the rule in many departments that subfields of the discipline enjoy greater intellectual rapport with subfields of other disciplines than with other subfields within the discipline. New informal groupings are occurring, while the traditional departmental authority in resource allocation and faculty evaluation remains unchanged.

Consequently, the academic department of the future may play a different role. The chairman of the department, who now sees himself as a manager, might act as a leader in a matrix organization (indeed, this is frequently the chairman's unofficial role at present). The function of the department would be defined by the curriculum, and traditional responsibilities concerned with instructional matters, such as teaching assignments, would remain in the department. The members of the department might engage in changing research groups within or outside the department, and those groups would have their own team leaders or project managers. Interdisciplinary teaching would be co-managed by the new breed of chairman and research team leader. Resource allocation at the dean or division level would take into account both instructional (departmental) and research (team) needs. Independent research need not be affected by the change, although departmental methods of accounting for the independent scholar might be developed. The objective would be modification of the organizational structure to correlate with changes in organizational behavior that are already occurring.

The changes in disciplines have been observed by the participants in this study; the full effect is yet to be seen. Over time, the restructuring of research may weaken the influence of traditional disciplines on the internal organization, and have an as yet unimagined effect on the prestige principle.

The twenty-first century may require a fundamental change in the structure and processes of the department-based faculty personnel system in the research university. The excellence that universities purport to seek is dependent upon the people of the organization; therefore, a focus on those people is necessary in order to achieve excellence. That focus is best sharpened in the context of contemporary human resource

management principles, and enhanced by the fair treatment and recognition of the worth of the individual professional that is inherent in those principles.

Caplow and McGee wrote, in the last sentence of their 1958 book:

We believe, perhaps too hopefully, that the recognition of the academic department as the primary unit of identification, the recognition of the university administration as responsible for controlling the development of competing disciplines within a single framework, and the insistence on explicit procedures to hold each participant in academic government within the sphere of his proper competence will lead to a situation in which all academic men can live in greater ease and with more hope of achievement. (*Marketplace*, p. 254–255)

The structuring of resource allocation that Caplow and McGee viewed as necessary is not now a point of contention—the academic department of today does not "own" its faculty positions. In other respects, their stratification is no longer so easily distinguished nor so clearly desirable. This replication of their study has found a different world for the research university, with blurring of distinctions—inside and out—and prominence of new values, and with personnel processes that in critical respects have fallen behind contemporary thinking. Caplow and McGee's work can be usefully extended in the 1990s and beyond through study of the organizational cultures of academia, and through action following study creating an environment in which all academic men and women "can live in greater ease and with more hope of achievement," and in which the research university will strengthen and grow in the new academic marketplace.

Appendix A

Methodology

Framework of the Study

Drawing from the Caplow and McGee recommendations stated in Chapter 1, I chose these focal categories of change or constancy:

a. *Market and policy.* Caplow and McGee described a strong seller's market in 1958, a unique market where differentiation was a factor but not a critical one. The participants in that academic labor market were overwhelmingly white and male.

Within the institution itself, Caplow and McGee found a severe conflict between the teaching and research needs of the university. Further, there appeared to be a lack of coherent management strategies to cope with the problems inherent in the faculty personnel system.

How does the market affect faculty personnel policies and practices today? Who are the participants in the market? Does the tension between research and teaching still exist or does it exist in so pronounced a form? Has "management" entered the academy?

b. *Recruitment methods.* The most-quoted feature of Caplow and McGee's study, and indeed a major contention, is that of closed, or preferential, hiring. Ingredients are "nepotistic" behavior, sponsorship, and doctoral prestige, aided by what they called "information screens," that is, an absence of information about jobs (on the part of the prospective candidates) and about candidates (on the part of the prospective employers).

Is hiring still closed, preferential? Has the broader advertising of positions in today's market altered the department's choice of candidates in quantity or quality?

c. *Selection.* Caplow and McGee found that publications were rarely read and that more than half the hirings in their sample took place without a campus interview. Letters of recommendation, however, were quite important in 1958. It was Caplow and McGee's maxim that a candidate is worth only what someone else thinks he is worth. Participation in the selection process, however, was relatively democratic in the 1950s, although Caplow and McGee noted the presence of autocratic chairmen.

What are the current procedures for assessing candidates? What counts most?

Has the change in the market structure intensified or diluted the prestige system? Who makes the selection decision—especially, does the university administration play a heavier role in hiring decisions or are academic departments successfully autonomous in hiring the people they want?

d. *Circumstances of termination.*   Caplow and McGee found that the majority of the vacancies in their sample were a consequence of resignation; they found mobility greatest for the assistant professor and least for the associate professor. Further, they identified "motives for migration"—prestige, security, and authority.

Is the incidence of denial of tenure as endemic to the assistant professor rank as it is thought to be? Has the mobility of associate and full professors changed? When people do move voluntarily, why do they do it and where do they go? What is the impact of their departure on the department?

Research Questions

By summarizing the indicators noted above, the following basic research questions were developed for the current study:

1. What are the effects of market and policy on the mobility of today's faculty?
2. What are the existing practices and criteria for discovering and evaluating faculty candidates?
3. How are selection decisions made?
4. What are the circumstances of faculty terminations?
5. What effect do the changed (or unchanged) conditions have on the academic organization?

Study Design

The study was designed as a replication of the Caplow and McGee study. Theodore Caplow (1982) provided a guide to replication based on his own Middletown study; the sense of his direction, translated loosely from the French, follows: He added some things not in the original study; he deleted some things that were in the original study; he reconsidered the fundamental problems in the Lynds (1929) study; and he also considered other later research throwing light on Middletown.

For this replication of the *Marketplace* study, the focus of the earlier study—the arts and sciences departments in the research university—was used, as was the general methodology. There were three departures from their design: (1) in the unit of analysis, (2) in the number of institutions studied, and (3) in the respondents.

1. The unit of analysis employed in the earlier study was a vacancy-and-replacement, in effect a sequence of events. The structural changes that have taken place in resource allocation over the years make that approach less logical today, and so I developed a design permitting the study of terminations and appointments separately. The unit of analysis thus became a specific personnel action. This has the advantage, besides convenience, of reversing the sequence

and viewing a chronological process: hiring, then firing (or leaving via some other route).

2. The original study involved nine major research universities, each of which was contacted for this study. Three of the universities refused to participate; two begged off because of internal crisis of some sort (not atypical in the sample), and one eminent research university simply declined in rather arrogant terms. (All three universities that denied access were private institutions.) Given the likelihood of an adequate number of interviews at the six remaining universities, I decided against attempting substitution for the three nonparticipants.

3. In an important change in emphasis, I broadened the scope of the study to include more subjects. Caplow and McGee confined their interviews to chairmen and "peers" (a peer being that person in the department closest in rank and age to the person who left), identifying the interviewees as "agents of the institution" (*Marketplace*, p. 28). I interviewed chairmen, peers (close colleagues) of the departed faculty members, and new appointees. Talking to new appointees added a dimension to the study that was quite useful in triangulation of data. Also, I was able to do a small amount of cross-checking by talking with a few new appointees who had left another institution in the sample, and a few emeritus professors, but these were not consistently developed data and were not used except to inform my own understanding. (A few quotes from emeritus professors are included.)

With these few exceptions, and considering ensuing research, the study was carried out in much the same manner as the earlier one. It might be noted here that as a woman I may have been treated differently from the men who conducted the interviews in 1957. No one tried to punch me in the nose, as happened to Reece McGee, nor was I called "stupid," another of his experiences. In comparing my interview data with his, which he very graciously made available to me, I find my interviews to be more civil and a bit more informative than those of the earlier era. This may, of course, simply reflect the fact that studies of universities and their faculties are no longer a novelty, whereas Professor McGee and his associate, Robb Taylor, were plowing new ground.

The Sample

The data were based on all terminations from tenured or tenure-track positions that occurred in arts and sciences departments of the six universities during the academic year 1983–84, and all appointments to tenured or tenure-track positions in the academic year 1984–85. Caplow and McGee studied 237 vacancies in the nine universities of their sample; my study investigated the circumstances of 167 terminations and 137 appointments, or a total of 304 personnel actions. The activity spread across fifty disciplines, as compared to thirty-two in the comparable six universities in the earlier study. (Only those six universities were used for all data comparisons.) Virtually all of the liberal arts disciplines were included, although not all on every campus. Economics, English, and physics were included in all six universities, and anthropology, chemistry, classical studies, history, philosophy, political science or government, and sociology in five of the six. Where the divisions of humanities, social sciences, and natural sciences were used, disciplines were assigned to divisions in accordance with their treatment at the specific university. For example, history may be found in the hu-

manities or the social sciences, linguistics in the humanities or social sciences, and psychology in the social sciences or natural sciences. Departments such as computer science and music have been included if they fall within a college of arts and sciences but have been excluded if they exist in a school of engineering or as a separate school. Administrative arrangements varied among the six universities: At some the chairmen of departments interacted directly with a dean of arts and sciences; at others the immediate relationship was with a divisional dean. In all cases the chairmen had available a written procedures manual setting out the administrative steps to be followed in making an appointment or forwarding a file for tenure consideration. Such written procedures did not exist when Caplow and McGee conducted their study.

The original researchers selected a convenience sample of major research universities, all members of the Association of American Universities, from which the six universities included in this study are drawn. Five of the institutions are "Research Universities I" according to the classifications developed by the Carnegie Commission of Higher Education (1976), that is:

The 50 leading universities in terms of federal financial support of academic science in at least two of the three academic years, 1972–73, 1973–74, and 1974–75, provided they awarded at least 50 Ph.D.'s . . . in 1973–74.

A sixth institution falls in the "Research Universities II" classification, defined as follows:

These universities were on the list of the 100 leading institutions in terms of federal financial support in at least two out of the above three years and awarded at least 50 Ph.D.'s . . . in 1973–74.

The research universities differ in their greater emphasis on research from "Doctoral-Granting Universities I," awarding forty or more doctorates or receiving at least $3 million in federal support; "Doctoral-Granting Universities II," awarding at least ten Ph.D.'s or emerging at that level; "Comprehensive Universities and Colleges I," including professional schools but lacking a doctoral program; "Comprehensive Universities and Colleges II," offering at least one professional or occupational program; and liberal arts colleges and other non-Ph.D.-awarding schools.

A number of studies, including Caplow and McGee's and this one, have used the major research university as a setting because it provides the primary training ground for new faculty members and also serves as a principal employer, thus establishing the norms for the profession. The research emphasis of these universities may translate into faculty hiring criteria, conditions of termination, and other personnel aspects that are somewhat different from schools in the other Carnegie classifications, hence limiting applicability of results. It should be noted here, however, that McGee (1971) found the hiring behavior in liberal arts colleges to be similar to that of research universities.

Within the research university classification, the six universities studied have diverse and representative characteristics: Two are in the Ivy League, two are in

the Big Ten, one is in California, one is in the Southwest; three are private, three are public; two are in metropolitan centers, two are in middle-sized cities, two are in small college towns. The six schools employed slightly more than ten thousand of the nation's faculty members in arts and sciences (they employed slightly more than seven thousand in 1958) and accounted for about 10 percent of the doctorates awarded in the United States in 1980. The departments represented in the sample contained a total of 3,302 faculty members.

The quality of the academic departments surveyed varied within and among institutions, with rankings ranging from one to fifty. The ranking measure used was "scholarly quality of program faculty," obtained by reputational survey, in Jones, Lindzey and Coggleshall (1982). Of ninety-five ranked departments, thirty-two were in the top ten and thirty-eight in the next ten (or seventy in the top twenty), eighteen were in the next ten and seven below that (or twenty-five below the top twenty). In three of the schools studied, virtually all of their departments that were represented in the sample and were included in the published rankings were found in the top twenty, two schools had a majority in the top twenty, and one had half of its departments below the top twenty. (Note that twenty-four of the fifty disciplines covered in the study were not included in the published rankings.)

Incidentally, Carnegie classification is not to be confused with department ranking; the institution with half of its departments below the top twenty is classified as a Research University I.

Information was furnished by 306 respondents from the six universities, compared to 310 from Caplow and McGee's nine universities in the earlier study. The information was obtained in 266 cases by personal interview, in six cases by telephone interview, and in the remaining thirty-four cases by mail.

Collecting the Data

Early in the summer of 1985 a letter and data form were sent to each of the participating schools requesting the following information about terminations and appointments: department and division; rank and tenure status of person who left and the reason for leaving (dismissal, resignation, retirement, death); rank and tenure status of the replacement; rank and tenure status of the appointee to a new position. Surprisingly, in our world of sophisticated administration and advanced technology, obtaining this list was far from easy. Caplow and McGee had commented, "Some universities took weeks to assemble the list, and errors were not uncommon" (*Marketplace*, p. 30). The lists I received were not wholly accurate on any of the campuses I visited. The advent of management information systems and offices of institutional research has apparently done little to alleviate the problem.

In addition, published materials on personnel procedures were requested, and also the designation of a contact person in the administration with whom I could arrange day-to-day operations during the campus visit. In one of the public universities and one of the private universities, a letter over an administrative signature was sent to department chairmen in advance of my visit, a helpful gesture that expedited appointment setting. In the other four universities, two public and two private, I obtained a letter upon arrival on campus that

I used as a letter of introduction. Many of the respondents were familiar with the Caplow and McGee book and all were interested in research, and so regardless of the degree of warmth in the official greeting, once I crossed the barrier of presenting my credentials to the administration, negotiating some kind of work space and message-taking, and getting on with it, I was well received on campus. Several of the faculty members with whom I talked were enthusiastic about my research, and the remainder ranged from tolerant to mildly interested. Exceptions were three chairmen—two at private universities and one at a public university—who refused to talk to me although two, when pressed, referred me to senior faculty members who had served as chairmen and proved to be excellent sources of information. In the third case I discovered the reason for reticence in an interview on another campus: deviations in procedure that were not known at the administration level, yet.

In several instances it was not possible to identify or contact peers; there were similar difficulties in reaching all of the new appointees, some of whom were on leave or had moved on to other jobs. Following is a table showing the response rate by institution, the second column showing the number of possible interviews and the third showing interviews conducted as a percentage of the possibilities.

Institution	N	Response Rate
A	54	85.2%
B	49	89.8%
C	75	74.7%
D	48	91.7%
E	56	89.3%
F	71	93.0%
Total	351	87.2%

The sample of 306 completed interviews consisted of seventy-seven assistant professors, forty-six associate professors, and 183 professors, in 131 departments. The sample included forty-nine women and twelve Asian, Black, and Hispanic minorities in fifty-one departments, as compared to Caplow and McGee's experience in the same schools of interviewing seventeen women and one Asian minority in twelve departments.

The interview guide used was essentially that used in the earlier study, with slight modifications in which Professor McGee assisted. For example, I asked a new question about the effect of campus affirmative action requirements on the search process and a question about comparative applicant pools. I deleted a few questions that were quite low-yield in the original study (e.g., a question about the school of thought of the departed faculty member, which Professor McGee had characterized to me as a "fishing expedition" on the researchers' part). I added a section to the interview guide of questions to be asked of the new appointee by paraphrasing questions from the section of the original form that posed questions to a chairman about a new appointment. In sum, the revised interview guide followed the logic of the earlier study to find out about the

people who left (who, how, why); to find out about the search (procedures, criteria, applicants); and to find out about the people who were appointed (who, how, why). I field-tested the new interview guide on my own campus and made minor adjustments as a result of the tests. (The 1958 and 1986 interview guides are included at the end of this appendix.)

Chairmen were asked about departures and appointments, peers were asked about departures and about appointments if they had useful knowledge about the latter, new appointees were asked about the circumstances of their own appointments. An interview with a chairman that encompassed both termination and appointment activity, or several of either types of activity, could take as long as an hour and a half. Peer interviews usually lasted less than an hour. Most new-appointee interviews were completed in half an hour. Because the questions were open-ended, designed to elicit individual comments rather than highly structured responses, the length of the interview varied to some extent with the degree of loquaciousness of the interviewee.

As to the actual process: Upon arriving on campus, I acquired a list of chairmen and a telephone and began calling to set up appointments. On every campus visited I was able to arrange at least one appointment on the afternoon of the first day. The chairman interview led to identification of peers and new appointees, and so some telephoning time was allotted every day during the first of the two weeks that I spent on each campus. All personal interviews were conducted in the faculty member's campus office or laboratory in as unobtrusive a manner as could be accomplished. Responses were recorded as nearly verbatim as possible on the interview form, and the interviews were dictated on cassettes at the end of each day. The tapes were subsequently transcribed onto disk and printed in rough draft form. I checked the drafts against the original interview notes and edited the disks, from which final copies were printed and photocopied. The photocopies were cut into sections, dividing the responses into preset groupings relating to research questions, and pasted on index cards.

While on site, I summarized responses to selected questions on spread sheets, and kept records of interviewee responsiveness and unusual circumstances or situations that would assist later interpretation of the interview data. After my return from a campus visit, I summarized descriptive statistics for the school, comparing Caplow and McGee results with mine, and elaborating on the statistics by using the response summaries prepared on site. Consequently, at the end of each site visit for the purpose of collecting field data, I had developed a familiarity with and a comprehensive view of the faculty personnel activity on that campus as well as some experience in handling the data.

Data Preparation

The advantage of using open-ended questions is that the information furnished by the respondents is less likely to be forced into preconceived pigeonholes constructed by the researcher. The disadvantage is the difficulty of making sense out of material that is not easily adaptable to quantification. In handling these data, I first made a list of "things I could count" and entered them on computer spreadsheets—for example, appointments by institution, discipline, and rank; terminations by type, institution, discipline, and rank; department ratings; department size. This step approximated that described by Caplow and McGee

(*Marketplace*, p. 37) and was substituted for the manual coding sheet used in the original study.

Next I applied categorical coding to the index cards, providing each with an eight-character code designating school, discipline, and role of interviewee; a two- or three-character code identifying disciplinary division, such as social sciences; a four-character code establishing type of action, with a fifth character for type of termination; and a four-character code for academic rank. All of the coding I used was non-numerical and relatively self-explanatory. This preliminary coding permitted aggregation of the interview data for analysis in various ways. It also facilitated a weighting process for certain questions by designating the role of the interviewee; for example, a new appointee would be more likely to provide the source of initial contact with the department than would the chairman, or a peer might have a better idea of why a colleague left to take another job.

At the next stage I was significantly guided by Miles and Huberman (1984), as well as my own background in literary and legal research, in coding themes within the interview data. I had noted certain repetitions during data collection (e.g., references to spouse employment) and established codes for about twenty recurring concepts. Some additional codes emerged from further familiarity with the responses as I worked with the data. Because my data were bounded by specific questions, this "fine-coding" task was not as complex as would be the case in ethnographic work.

Concomitant with fine-coding was content analysis of the data to furnish discrete quantifiable items. Among these were such determinations as the level at which an academic opening was defined, and the level at which a candidate was selected, whether by provost, dean, chairman, department members, or one or more acting in concert. Content analysis also permitted development of classifications such as negative or positive response.

And so, quoting Theodore Caplow and Reece McGee: "In sum, the methods used were the simplest which would serve" (*Marketplace*, p. 39).

Interview Guide: 1958

FACULTY MOBILITY STUDY   **Form   4**

Vacancy: A_____

Name   B_____

Position

Department

Salary

Duties (% estimate)

Date of Termination

Age

Replacement:

Name

Position

Salary

Duties (% estimates)

Age

Respondent:

Name

Position

Date of Interview

Time

Recept:

Yield   Interviewer _____

A. THE VACANCY

1. When was the vacancy foreseen? (dates of first rumor, known offer, known acceptance)
2. Were any efforts made to hold him here? (how, what outcome, if not, why not)
3. What attracted him most about the new position?
   FOR RETIREMENTS—What was his reaction to retirement?

4. Were there unsatisfactory elements in his position here?

5. How does his new position compare? (rank, salary, function, opportunities, perquisites)

6. How did he come to get an offer from there?
   FOR RETIREMENTS—Did he have any opportunities offered when he retired?

7. Is he satisfied with his new position?

8. Was there any formal send-off by the department when he left?

9. How long had he been there?

10. Would you say that his departure means a real change for the department?

11. Is there a particular professional viewpoint with which he is identified? (identify opposing school also)

12. Was he involved in active collaboration with any of his colleagues? (who, what rank)

13. Did you ever work with him yourself? (if applicable)

14. Was he well acquainted outside the department? (within the institution)

15. Are any of his students likely to follow him?
    FOR RETIREMENTS—Are any of his students still working with him?

16. Do you think he has reached the peak of his productivity as yet?
    FOR RETIREMENTS—When did he reach the peak of his productivity?

B. THE SEARCH

17. Did you consider a direct replacement to be necessary?

18. What were the first steps taken? (when, by whom, in what form)

19. Were the duties and responsibilities of the new position determined in advance?

20. How many names were mentioned for consideration?
    How many became active candidates?

21. What credentials were submitted? (oral recommendations, written recommendations, curricula vitae, publications unread, publications read, interviews, visits)

22. What were the desirable qualifications? Were they set down in writing? If not, did you have a clear idea of what was wanted?

23. What were the specific procedures for evaluation of the candidates?

24. On what basis was the choice made between the candidate finally selected and the closest runner-up?

C. THE REPLACEMENT

25. Through whom was the first contact made?

26. Did the candidate have any prior contact with the department or the university? (double-check)

27. How did his old position compare? (rank, salary, function, opportunities, perquisites)

28. Why was he willing to move?

29. How were his qualifications evaluated? (relate to questions 21 and 23)

30. Who was consulted before the offer was made?

31. Who took what formal action when the offer was made? (in detail)

32. Was there any bidding process? Were there any special terms and conditions? Was there further consultation?

33. When and how was the offer made? (copies, if possible)

34. When and how was the acceptance received? When did the appointee take up his duties?

35. How about opportunities for outside consultation work?

36. Do you expect this appointment to have any long-run effect on the department's program as a whole?

37. Can you foresee the circumstances of the next major appointment in the department? Are there any balancing factors to be considered?

38. Will this appointment affect the policy of later appointments?

39. Name of colleague of nearest rank and age.

40. How would you rate the national reputation of this department in its own field? (among the first five, better than average of major institutions, average, poorer than average)

41. How has the job market in this field changed in the past five years?

Postscript

Remarks

Interview Guide: 1986

FACULTY MOBILITY STUDY

Vacancy: File I.D.:

Position: *School:*

Date of termination: *Dept:*

Age:
                             Jones ranking
First appointment date: (Measure 08):

Replacement/New Hire:

Position:

Age:

Date of Ph.D.:

Respondent:

Name:

Position:

Date of interview:

Time:

Receptivity:

Yield:

A. THE VACANCY

1. When was the vacancy foreseen? (dates of first rumor, known offer, known acceptance; if involuntary, circumstances)

2. Were any efforts made to hold him/her here? (how, what outcome, if not why not)

3. What attracted him/her most about the new position?
   FOR RETIREMENTS—What was his/her reaction to retirement?
   Did he/she take early retirement? If so, what was the incentive to do so?
   Is he/she still professionally active?

4. Were there unsatisfactory elements in his/her position here?

5. How does his/her new position compare? (rank, salary, function, opportunities, perquisites)

6. How did he/she come to get an offer from there?
   FOR RETIREMENTS—Did he/she have any opportunities offered when he/she retired?

7. Is he/she satisfied with his/her new position?

8. Would you say that his/her departure means a real change for the department?

9. Was he/she involved in active collaboration with any of his/her colleagues? (who, what rank)

10. Was he/she well acquainted outside the department? (within the institution, outside the institution)

B. THE SEARCH

11. Did you consider a direct replacement to be necessary?

12. What were the first steps taken? (when, by whom, in what form; determination of need, authorization to recruit, communication to prospective candidates)

13. Were the duties and responsibilities of the new position determined in advance?

14. How many applicants did you have for the position? (estimate recruitment source)
    How many on "short list"? (recruitment source, schools; women, minorities)
    How many visited? (recruitment source, schools; women, minorities)

15. What credentials were submitted?

16. What were the qualifications for the position? Were they set down in writing? If not, did you have a clear idea of what was wanted?

17. What were the specific procedures for evaluation of the candidates at each screening step? (criteria, application of criteria, participants in evaluation; include interview process)

18. On what basis was the choice made between the candidate finally selected and the closest runner-up?
    Was he/she your first choice?
    What was the successful candidate's recruitment source, school?

19. How was your search affected by affirmative action requirements? Were more women and/or minority candidates actually produced?

20. Was your search affected by recommendations or guidelines of your professional association (AEA, MLA, etc.)?

21. Compared with the way recruiting was done 15–20 years ago, do your present search procedures produce more candidates? Different candidates? Better candidates?

C. THE REPLACEMENT

22. Through whom was the first contact made?
23. Did the candidate have any prior contact with the department or the university? (inbreeding–outbreeding)
24. How did his/her old position compare? (rank, salary, function, opportunities, perquisites)
25. Why was he/she willing to move?
26. What attracted him/her to this department?
27. How was the offer made? (in detail; who was consulted, etc.)
28. Was there any negotiation with candidate or administration? Were there any special terms and conditions? Was there further consultation?
29. Are there any budgeting arrangements for special allocation of funds to hire exceptional people? Blacks or other minorities? Women? Other? (used in this instance? ever used in this department?)
30. Do you expect this appointment to have any long-run effect on the department's program as a whole?
31. Can you foresee the circumstances of the next major appointment in the department? Are there any balancing factors to be considered?
32. Will this appointment affect the policy of later appointments?
33. [deleted]
34. How has the job market in this field changed in the past five years? How is it going to change in the next five years?
35. Is the recruiting activity reported for 1985 appointments typical? (different the previous year or the year before, different this year; how, why)

D. NEW APPOINTEE

36. How did the job opening first come to your attention?
37. Did you have any prior contact with the department or the university?
38. How did your old position compare with this one? (rank, salary, function, opportunities, perquisites)
39. Why were you willing to move?
40. What attracted you to this department?
41. What credentials did you submit for consideration?
42. What were the procedures used during the evaluation process? (known or experienced)
43. How was the offer actually communicated to you?
44. Was there any negotiation involved in your acceptance?
45. Is this the job you wanted? How many other interviews did you have? (where, offers)
46. How would you rate the national reputation of this department? (among the

first five, better than average of major institutions, average, poorer than average)

47. How has the job market in your field changed in the past five years? How is it going to change in the next five years?

REMARKS:

Appendix B

Data Comparison

The following schedules provide comparisons of data from the 1958 and 1986 studies on several dimensions, as listed below:

Ia. Appointments 1955–57

Ib. Appointments 1984–85

IIa. Dismissals 1955–57

IIb. Dismissals 1983–84

IIIa. Resignations 1955–57

IIIb. Resignations 1983–84

IVa. Retirements 1955–57

IVb. Retirements 1983–84

V. Respondents 1958, 1986

VI. Disciplines Represented 1958, 1986

VII. Data Summary by Institution 1958, 1986

VIII. Department Size by Institution 1986

IX. Department Ranking 1986

Ia. Appointments 1955-57

Number of Actions

	Public University A			Private University B			Public University C			Private University D			Private University E			Public University F		
	Asst	Assc	Prof	Asst	Assc	Prof	Asst	Assc	Prof	Asst	Assc	Prof	Asst	Assc	Prof	Asst	Assc	Prof
HUMANITIES																		
Art																		
Classics																2		
Decrtv Art	1	1																
Drama/Thea	1			1														
English	1		1	1	1				1							1		
Fine Arts								1										
German	1			1						1								
Ital/French							2											
Music		1		1									1					
Nr East St	1																	
Philosophy	1			1														
Rom St/Lang				1	1					1								
Slavic Lang														1		2		
Span & Port																		
Speech	1																	
Sub-total	7	2	1	6	2	0	2	1	1	2	0	0	1	1	0	5	0	0

Ia. Appointments 1955-57

Number of Actions

	Public University A			Private University B			Public University C			Private University D			Private University E			Public University F		
	Asst	Assc	Prof	Asst	Assc	Prof	Asst	Assc	Prof	Asst	Assc	Prof	Asst	Assc	Prof	Asst	Assc	Prof
SOCIAL SCI																		
Anthropology																2		
Economics		2		1			1			3			2			1		
Geography							1			1				1				
History	1	2							1	1	1		1			1		
Home Econ							1											
Journalism							1											
Polit Sci	1											1						
Psychology	1						2					1						
Social Svc							1											
Sociology																		
Sub-total	3	4	0	1	0	0	7	0	1	5	1	2	3	1	0	4	0	0

Ia. Appointments 1955-57

	Number of Actions																	
	Public University A			Private University B			Public University C			Private University D			Private University E			Public University F		
	Asst	Assc	Prof	Asst	Assc	Prof	Asst	Assc	Prof	Asst	Assc	Prof	Asst	Assc	Prof	Asst	Assc	Prof
NATURAL SCI																		
Astronomy				1						1			1					1
Biochem		1																
Biol Sci								1										
Botany													2					
Chemistry	1			1				1										
Geology	1			1									2					
Home Econ														1			1	
Mathematics	1	1								2	1							
Physics	2			2			3						1	1		1		
Zoology							1									1	1	
Sub-total	5	1	1	5	0	0	3	0	1	4	1	0	3	1	1	4	1	1
TOTAL	11	7	2	12	2	0	12	1	3	11	2	2	7	3	1	13	1	1

Ia. Appointments 1955-57

Totals

HUMANITIES	Asst	Assc	Prof	All
Art	0	0	0	0
Classics	2	0	0	2
Decrtv Art	0	1	0	1
Drama/Thea	2	1	0	3
English	4	1	1	6
Fine Arts	0	1	0	1
German	3	0	0	3
Ital/French	2	0	0	2
Music	2	0	1	3
Nr East St	1	0	0	1
Philosophy	2	0	0	2
Rom St/Lang	4	2	0	6
Slavic Lang	0	0	0	0
Span & Port	0	0	0	0
Speech	1	0	0	1
Sub-total	23	6	2	31

SOCIAL SCI	Asst	Assc	Prof	All
Anthropology	3	0	0	3
Economics	7	2	0	9
Geography	1	1	1	3
History	4	3	1	8
Home Econ	1	0	0	1
Journalism	1	0	0	1
Polit Sci	1	0	1	2
Psychology	4	0	0	4
Social Svc	1	0	0	1
Sociology	0	0	0	0
Sub-total	23	6	3	32

NATURAL SCI	Asst	Assc	Prof	All
Astronomy	2	0	0	2
Biochem	0	0	1	1
Biol Sci	1	0	0	1
Botany	2	0	0	2
Chemistry	2	0	0	2
Geology	3	0	0	3
Home Econ	1	1	0	2
Mathematics	3	2	0	5
Physics	6	1	1	8
Zoology	0	0	2	2
Sub-total	20	4	4	28

	Asst	Assc	Prof	All
TOTAL	66	16	9	91

1b. Appointments 1984-85

Number of Actions

SOCIAL SCI	Public University A Asst	Assc	Prof	Private University B Asst	Assc	Prof	Public University C Asst	Assc	Prof	Private University D Asst	Assc	Prof	Private University E Asst	Assc	Prof	Public University F Asst	Assc	Prof
Afro-Am St	1																	
Anthropology	1							1		1								
Asian-Am St																		
Economics				1			3			2						1		
Geography							1			1			1			1		
Govt/Pol Sc				1			2			1						1		
History							1	2			1		3			3		
Home Econ							1											
Linguistics	1							1										
Psychology							2						2			1		
Region Sci									1				1					
Sociology	1			1						1			1					
Telecomm		1				1	1					1			1			1
Sub-total	4	1	0	3	0	1	11	4	1	5	1	1	8	0	1	7	0	1

1b. Appointments 1984-85

Number of Actions

	Public University A			Private University B			Public University C			Private University D			Private University E			Public University F		
HUMANITIES	Asst	Assc	Prof	Asst	Assc	Prof	Asst	Assc	Prof	Asst	Assc	Prof	Asst	Assc	Prof	Asst	Assc	Prof
Amer Civ										1								
Art History	1			1							1				1			
Classics	1							1						1				
Comp Lit	1																	
Drama/Thea	1				1													
English	1				2					2			2					
Fine Arts							1				2			1				
German																		
History	1																	
Ital/French	1																	
Linguistics										1								
Modern Lang										1								
Music																		
Nr East St	1				1													
Orien/As St							1											
Philosophy				1				2		2						2		
Relig St							2											
Rhetoric																		
Rom St/Lang										1								
Russian Lit																		
Span & Port	1												1					
Sub-total	6	1	0	6	0	4	1	0	1	3	3	8	1	0	3	0	0	2

1b. Appointments 1984-85

Number of Actions

NATURAL SCI	Public University A (Asst Assc Prof)			Private University B (Asst Assc Prof)			Public University C (Asst Assc Prof)			Private University D (Asst Assc Prof)			Private University E (Asst Assc Prof)			Public University F (Asst Assc Prof)		
Astronomy							1										1	
Molec Biol	2							1	1									
Chemistry									1	2		1		1		2		
Comp Sci				1												3		
Ecol & Sys																		
Geology							1											1
Home Econ									2									1
Mathematics			1				1					1						
Microb & Imm			1									1						
Nrbiol & Beh						1					1							
Physio & Ana	1																	
Physical Ed	1																	
Physics							1	1		3	1		1				1	
Psychology										1								
Statistics	1																	
Zoology													1					
Sub-total	5	0	4	1	0	0	5	2	2	4	2	1	0	1	1	10	1	2
TOTAL	15	2	4	10	0	0	20	7	3	10	6	5	21	1	2	20	1	5

156

1b. Appointments 1984-85

Totals

HUMANITIES	Asst	Assc	Prof	All
Amer Civ	1	0	0	1
Art History	2	1	1	4
Classics	4	0	0	4
Comp Lit	1	0	0	1
Drama/Thea	2	0	1	3
English	4	1	2	7
Fine Arts	0	1	2	3
German	0	0	0	0
History	1	0	0	1
Ital/French	1	0	0	1
Linguistics	1	0	0	1
Modern Lang	0	0	0	0
Music	1	0	0	1
Nr East St	1	0	1	2
Orien/As St	3	0	0	3
Philosophy	2	2	2	6
Relig St	2	0	0	2
Rhetoric	0	0	0	0
Rom St/Lang	1	0	0	1
Russian Lit	0	0	0	0
Span & Port	1	1	0	2
Sub-total	28	6	9	43

SOCIAL SCI	Asst	Assc	Prof	All
Afro-Am St	1	0	0	1
Anthropology	3	1	0	4
Asian-Am St	0	0	0	0
Economics	8	2	0	10
Geography	2	0	1	3
Govt/Pol Sc	5	2	0	7
History	5	0	1	6
Home Econ	2	0	0	2
Linguistics	3	0	1	4
Psychology	3	0	0	3
Region Sci	0	0	0	0
Sociology	5	1	2	8
Telecomm	1	0	0	1
Sub-total	38	6	5	49

NATURAL SCI	Asst	Assc	Prof	All
Astronomy	2	0	0	2
Molec Biol	4	1	1	6
Chemistry	3	1	2	6
Comp Sci	4	0	0	4
Ecol & Sys	0	0	0	0
Geology	1	0	1	2
Home Econ	2	0	1	3
Mathematics	1	1	2	4
Microb & Imm	0	0	1	1
Nrbiol & Beh	2	0	0	2
Physio & Ana	1	0	0	1
Physical Ed	1	0	0	1
Physics	6	2	0	8
Psychology	1	0	0	1
Statistics	1	0	1	2
Zoology	1	0	1	2
Sub-total	30	5	10	45

TOTAL	96	17	24	137

157

IIa. Dismissals 1955-57

Number of Actions

	Public University A			Private University B			Public University C			Private University D			Private University E			Public University F		
	Asst	Assc	Prof	Asst	Assc	Prof	Asst	Assc	Prof	Asst	Assc	Prof	Asst	Assc	Prof	Asst	Assc	Prof
HUMANITIES																		
Art																		
Classics																1		
Decrtv Art	1																	
Drama/Thea	1																	
English	2						1											
Fine Arts										1								
German	1			1														
Ital/French																		
Music																		
Nr East St																		
Philosophy	1																	
Rom St/Lang																2		
Slavic Lang																1		
Span & Port																		
Speech	3																	
Sub-total	9	0	0	1	0	0	1	0	0	1	0	0	0	0	0	4	0	0

IIa. Dismissals 1955-57

Number of Actions

	Public University A			Private University B			Public University C			Private University D			Private University E			Public University F		
	Asst	Assc	Prof	Asst	Assc	Prof	Asst	Assc	Prof	Asst	Assc	Prof	Asst	Assc	Prof	Asst	Assc	Prof
SOCIAL SCI																		
Anthropology																2		
Economics																2		
Geography																		
History	2												1					
Home Econ																		
Journalism																		
Polit Sci																		
Psychology	1																1	
Social Svc																		
Sociology																		
Sub-total	3	0	0	0	0	0	0	0	0	0	0	0	1	0	0	4	1	0

159

IIa. Dismissals 1955-57

Number of Actions

	Public University A			Private University B			Public University C			Private University D			Private University E			Public University F		
	Asst	Assc	Prof	Asst	Assc	Prof	Asst	Assc	Prof	Asst	Assc	Prof	Asst	Assc	Prof	Asst	Assc	Prof
NATURAL SCI																		
Astronomy																		
Biochem					1													
Biol Sci																		
Botany																		
Chemistry										1								
Geology														1				
Home Econ																		
Mathematics										1								
Physics				1			1						3					
Psychology													1					
Zoology																		
Sub-total	0	0	0	1	1	0	1	0	0	2	0	0	5	0	0	1	0	0
TOTAL	12	0	0	2	1	0	1	0	0	3	0	0	5	0	0	1	0	0

IIa. Dismissals 1955-57

Totals

HUMANITIES

	Asst	Assc	Prof	All
Art	0	0	0	0
Classics	1	0	0	1
Decrtv Art	1	0	0	1
Drama/Thea	1	0	0	1
English	4	0	0	4
Fine Arts	0	0	0	0
German	2	0	0	2
Ital/French	0	0	0	0
Music	0	0	0	0
Nr East St	0	0	0	0
Philosophy	1	0	0	1
Rom St/Lang	2	0	0	2
Slavic Lang	1	0	0	1
Span & Port	0	0	0	0
Speech	3	0	0	3
Sub-total	16	0	0	16

SOCIAL SCI

	Asst	Assc	Prof	All
Anthropology	2	0	0	2
Economics	2	0	0	2
Geography	0	0	0	0
History	3	0	0	3
Home Econ	0	0	0	0
Journalism	0	0	0	0
Polit Sci	0	0	0	0
Psychology	1	1	0	2
Social Svc	0	0	0	0
Sociology	0	0	0	0
Sub-total	8	1	0	9

NATURAL SCI

	Asst	Assc	Prof	All
Astronomy	0	1	0	1
Biochem	0	0	0	0
Biol Sci	0	0	0	0
Botany	0	0	0	0
Chemistry	1	0	0	1
Geology	1	0	0	1
Home Econ	0	0	0	0
Mathematics	1	0	0	1
Physics	5	0	0	5
Psychology	0	0	0	0
Zoology	0	1	0	0
Sub-total	8	2	0	9

	Asst	Assc	Prof	All
TOTAL	33	2	0	35

IIb. Dismissals 1983-84

Number of Actions

	Public University A			Private University B			Public University C			Private University D			Private University E			Public University F		
	Asst	Assc	Prof	Asst	Assc	Prof	Asst	Assc	Prof	Asst	Assc	Prof	Asst	Assc	Prof	Asst	Assc	Prof
SOCIAL SCI																		
Afro-Am St																		
Anthropology																		
Asian-Am St																		
Economics	1												2					
Geography																1		
Govt/Pol Sc																		
History													2			1		
Linguistics																		
Psychology													2			2		
Region Sci													1					
Sociology																		
Sub-total	1	0	0	0	0	0	0	0	0	0	0	0	7	0	0	4	0	0

IIb. Dismissals 1983-84

Number of Actions

	Public University A			Private University B			Public University C			Private University D			Private University E			Public University F		
	Asst	Assc Prof		Asst	Assc Prof		Asst	Assc Prof		Asst	Assc Prof		Asst	Assc Prof		Asst	Assc Prof	
HUMANITIES																		
Afro-Am Stud										1								
Amer Civ													1					
Art History													1					
Classics																1		
Comp Lit																		
Drama/Thea				1														
English				1						2			1			3		
German																		
History																		
Ital/French																		
Linguistics																		
Modern Lang																		
Music													2					
Nr East St																		
Orien/As St													1					
Philosophy										1						2		
Relig St																		
Rhetoric	1																	
Rom St/Lang																		
Russian Lit																		
Span & Port							1											
Sub-total	1	0	0	0	0	0	1	0	0	4	0	0	6	0	0	6	0	0

IIb. Dismissals 1983-84

	Public University A		Private University B		Public University C		Private University D		Private University E		Public University F	
	Asst	Assc Prof	Asst	Assc Prof	Asst	Assc Prof	Asst	Assc Prof	Asst	Assc Prof	Asst	Assc Prof
NATURAL SCI												
Astronomy												
Molec Biol												
Chemistry			1		2							
Comp Sci									1			
Ecol & Sys												
Geology							1					
Home Econ											1	
Mathematics											2	
Microb & Imm												
Nrbiol & Beh											1	
Physio & Ana												
Physical Ed												
Physics											1	
Statistics												
Zoology											1	
Sub-total	0	0	1	0	2	0	1	0	1	0	6	0
TOTAL	2	0	1	0	4	0	5	0	15	0	16	0

IIb. Dismissals 1983-84

Totals

HUMANITIES	Asst	Assc	Prof	All
Afro-Am Stud	1	0	0	1
Amer Civ	1	0	0	1
Art History	0	0	0	0
Classics	2	0	0	2
Comp Lit	0	0	0	0
Drama/Thea	0	0	0	0
English	7	0	0	7
German	0	0	0	0
History	0	0	0	0
Ital/French	0	0	0	0
Linguistics	0	0	0	0
Modern Lang	0	0	0	0
Music	2	0	0	2
Nr East St	0	0	0	0
Orien/As St	1	0	0	1
Philosophy	3	0	0	3
Relig St	0	0	0	0
Rhetoric	1	0	0	1
Rom St/Lang	0	0	0	0
Russian Lit	0	0	0	0
Span & Port	1	0	0	1
Sub-total	19	0	0	19

SOCIAL SCI	Asst	Assc	Prof	All
Afro-Am St	0	0	0	0
Anthropology	0	0	0	0
Asian-Am St	0	0	0	0
Economics	3	0	0	3
Geography	1	0	0	1
Govt/Pol Sc	0	0	0	0
History	3	0	0	3
Linguistics	0	0	0	0
Psychology	2	0	0	2
Region Sci	2	0	0	2
Sociology	1	0	0	1
Sub-total	12	0	0	12

NATURAL SCI	Asst	Assc	Prof	All
Astronomy	0	0	0	0
Molec Biol	0	0	0	0
Chemistry	3	0	0	3
Comp Sci	1	0	0	1
Ecol & Sys	0	0	0	0
Geology	1	0	0	1
Home Econ	1	0	0	1
Mathematics	3	0	0	3
Microb & Imm	1	0	0	1
Nrbiol & Beh	0	0	0	0
Physio & Ana	0	0	0	0
Physical Ed	0	0	0	0
Physics	1	0	0	1
Statistics	0	0	0	0
Zoology	1	0	0	1
Sub-total	12	0	0	12

TOTAL	43	0	0	43

IIIa. Resignations 1955-57

Number of Actions

	Public University A			Private University B			Public University C			Private University D			Private University E			Public University F		
	Asst	Assc	Prof	Asst	Assc	Prof	Asst	Assc	Prof	Asst	Assc	Prof	Asst	Assc	Prof	Asst	Assc	Prof
HUMANITIES																		
Art		1																
Classics																		
Decrtv Art																		
Drama/Thea	1			1				1										
English				1					1								1	
Fine Arts							1	1										
German							1			1								
Ital/French										1								
Music					1								1					
Nr East St	1																	
Philosophy				1														
Rom St/Lang				1						1					1			
Slavic Lang						1						1						
Span & Port						1						1						
Speech																		
Sub-total	2	1	0	4	1	2	2	2	1	3	0	2	1	0	1	0	1	0

IIIa. Resignations 1955-57

Number of Actions

	Public University A			Private University B			Public University C			Private University D			Private University E			Public University F		
	Asst	Assc	Prof	Asst	Assc	Prof	Asst	Assc	Prof	Asst	Assc	Prof	Asst	Assc	Prof	Asst	Assc	Prof
SOCIAL SCI																		
Anthropology																		
Economics	1	1								3			1	1				
Geography							1						1					
History												1			1	1		
Home Econ																		
Journalism							1											
Polit Sci										1			1					
Psychology							2				1							
Social Svc							1											
Sociology																		
Sub-total	1	1	0	0	0	0	5	0	0	4	1	1	3	1	1	1	0	0

167

IIIa. Resignations 1955-57

Number of Actions

	Public University A			Private University B			Public University C			Private University D			Private University E			Public University F		
	Asst	Assc	Prof	Asst	Assc	Prof	Asst	Assc	Prof	Asst	Assc	Prof	Asst	Assc	Prof	Asst	Assc	Prof
NATURAL SCI																		
Astronomy																		
Biochem																		
Biol Sci																		
Botany											2							
Chemistry				1					1					1				
Geology				1														
Home Econ															2		1	1
Mathematics							2											
Physics		1			1	1		1				2		1				
Psychology																		
Zoology							1											
Sub-total	0	1	0	2	1	1	3	1	1	0	2	2	0	2	2	0	1	1
TOTAL	3	3	1	6	2	3	7	4	1	10	8	3	4	3	2	4	1	2

IIIa. Resignations 1955-57

HUMANITIES	Asst	Assc	Prof	All
Art	0	1	0	1
Classics	0	0	0	0
Decrtv Art	0	0	0	0
Drama/Thea	2	1	0	3
English	2	1	1	4
Fine Arts	1	1	1	3
German	1	0	1	2
Ital/French	0	0	0	0
Music	1	1	0	2
Nr East St	1	0	0	1
Philosophy	1	0	1	2
Rom St/Lang	2	0	2	4
Slavic Lang	1	0	0	1
Span & Port	0	0	0	0
Speech	0	0	0	0
Sub-total	12	5	6	23

Totals

SOCIAL SCI	Asst	Assc	Prof	All
Anthropology	1	1	0	2
Economics	4	1	1	6
Geography	2	0	1	3
History	1	1	0	2
Home Econ	0	0	0	0
Journalism	1	0	0	1
Polit Sci	1	3	1	5
Psychology	3	2	0	5
Social Svc	1	0	0	1
Sociology	0	0	0	0
Sub-total	14	8	3	25

NATURAL SCI	Asst	Assc	Prof	All
Astronomy	0	0	0	0
Biochem	0	0	0	0
Biol Sci	0	2	0	2
Botany	0	1	0	1
Chemistry	2	0	0	2
Geology	1	0	1	2
Home Econ	2	0	1	3
Mathematics	2	0	0	2
Physics	1	4	1	6
Psychology	0	0	0	0
Zoology	0	1	0	1
Sub-total	8	8	3	19

	Asst	Assc	Prof	All
TOTAL	34	21	12	67

IIIb. Resignations 1983-84

Number of Actions

HUMANITIES	Public University A			Private University B			Public University C			Private University D			Private University E			Public University F		
	Asst	Assc Prof	Assc Prof	Asst	Assc Prof	Assc Prof	Asst	Assc Prof	Assc Prof	Asst	Assc Prof	Assc Prof	Asst	Assc Prof	Assc Prof	Asst	Assc Prof	Assc Prof
Amer Civ																		
Art History				1														
Classics														1				
Comp Lit	1																	
Drama/Thea	1																	
English											1			1		1		
German															1	1		
History																		
Ital/French																		1
Linguistics																		
Modern Lang				1														
Music																		
Nr East St				1														
Orien/As St													1					
Philosophy	1												1					
Relig St													1					
Rhetoric																		
Rom St/Lang							1											
Russian Lit				1														
Span & Port									1									
Sub-total	3	0	0	4	0	0	1	0	1	0	1	0	2	2	1	2	0	1

170

IIIb. Resignations 1983-84

	Number of Actions																	
	Public University A			Private University B			Public University C			Private University D			Private University E			Public University F		
	Asst	Assc	Prof	Asst	Assc	Prof	Asst	Assc	Prof	Asst	Assc	Prof	Asst	Assc	Prof	Asst	Assc	Prof
SOCIAL SCI																		
Afro-Am St																		
Anthropology	1	1		1			1				1							
Asian-Am St	1																	
Economics				1			1						6			3	1	
Geography										1						1	1	
Govt/Pol Sc										1	2		2			1	1	
History							1				2				1	2		
Home Econ																		
Linguistics																		2
Psychology				2												1	1	
Region Sci															1			
Sociology							1									1		
Speech Comm							1											
Sp & Hrg Sci							1											
Sub-total	1	2	0	4	0	0	3	0	0	4	2	0	8	0	2	7	3	3

IIIb. Resignations 1983-84

Number of Actions

	Public University A			Private University B			Public University C			Private University D			Private University E			Public University F		
	Asst	Assc	Prof	Asst	Assc	Prof	Asst	Assc	Prof	Asst	Assc	Prof	Asst	Assc	Prof	Asst	Assc	Prof
NATURAL SCI																		
Astronomy																		
Molec Biol							1	1										
Chemistry								1										1
Comp Sci							2											
Ecol & Sys				1														
Geology								1										
Home Econ													1	1			1	1
Mathematics							1	1										
Microb & Imm																		
Nrbiol & Beh																		
Physio & Ana																		
Physical Ed																		
Physics								1			1			1			1	
Statistics																		
Zoology																		
Sub-total	0	0	0	1	0	0	4	5	0	0	1	0	0	2	0	0	2	2
TOTAL	4	2	0	8	4	0	4	9	0	0	1	4	2	3	0	11	5	6